SpringerBriefs in Computer Science

Series Editors

Stan Zdonik
Peng Ning
Shashi Shekhar
Jonathan Katz
Xindong Wu
Lakhmi C. Jain
David Padua
Xuemin Shen
Borko Furht
V. S. Subrahmanian
Martial Hebert
Katsushi Ikeuchi
Bruno Siciliano

For further volumes:
http://www.springer.com/series/10028

Hala ElAarag

Web Proxy Cache Replacement Strategies

Simulation, Implementation, and Performance Evaluation

With Contributions by Sam Romano and Jake Cobb

 Springer

Hala ElAarag
Department of Mathematics
   and Computer Science
Stetson University
DeLand, FL
USA

ISSN 2191-5768   ISSN 2191-5776   (electronic)
ISBN 978-1-4471-4892-0   ISBN 978-1-4471-4893-7   (eBook)
DOI 10.1007/978-1-4471-4893-7
Springer London Heidelberg New York Dordrecht

Library of Congress Control Number: 2012954855

Printed on acid-free paper

Springer is part of Springer Science+Business Media (www.springer.com)

To my loving parents, husband, and children

Preface

The need for this book stems from the sheer amount of modern web traffic coupled with increases in cacheable, bandwidth-consuming multimedia objects. In this book, we provide the most comprehensive study for proxy cache replacement strategies. We categorize these strategies into four categories; recency-based, frequency-based, recency/frequency-based, and function-based. We provide a quantitative comparison of cache replacement strategies on the category level and then compare the best strategies of each category based on very important performance metrics. We then diverge from these replacement policies by constructing a model, represented in the weights and structure of a neural network, from actual web traffic. This approach has the advantage of incorporating subtle traffic pattern information which may be difficult for a human to discern when designing a top-down algorithm. Furthermore, we provide a single method which is capable of creating multiple models; this allows models to be created which target localized traffic patterns as well as general ones. We first provide the simulation architecture, setup, parameters, and results of this novel technique then we explain the implementation details in the Squid proxy server.

This book is based on a number of my publications co-authored with my students Sam Romano, now a software engineer at Google and Jake Cobb, now a Ph.D. student at Georgia Institute of Technology. I would like to thank them both for their contributions to this research. I would like to thank the anonymous reviewers of *Simulation: Transactions of the Society for Modeling and Simulation International*, Sage Publication, *The Journal of Systems and Software*, Elsevier, and *Neural Computing and Applications*, Springer-Verlag, for their comments and critique that helped to improve the quality of this research. I would also like to thank the staff members of Springer, Wayne Wheeler for introducing me to the Springer Brief series and Simon Rees, for the follow up through the preparation of this book.

Last, but not least, I am deeply grateful to my family for their continuous support and encouragement.

Contents

Chapter 1
Introduction

Keywords Web proxy servers · Proxy cache · Cache replacement strategies · Neural networks · Squid proxy server

With the debut of Web 2.0, many researchers are interested in studying their workload characteristics in order to design more efficient servers. YouTube is an example of a very popular Web 2.0 site, and hence, it was the choice for many to conduct such research [1]. Gill et al. [1] conducted an extensive analysis of YouTube workload and observed 25-million YouTube transactions over a three-month period that included the downloads of 600,000 videos. They compared traditional Web workload characteristics to that of YouTube and found many similarities. They concluded that traffic characterization of YouTube suggests that caching popular video files on Web proxy servers reduces network traffic and increases scalability of YouTube servers [1].

User-perceived delay results from both overload of individual servers and network congestion. Proxy caches are used to address both issues by attempting to serve requests locally. There are several decisions that must be made such as cache placement and replacement. Our main focus will be the cache replacement problem, the process of evicting objects in the cache to make room for new objects, applied to Web proxy servers. Proxy servers want to serve as many objects from the cache as possible, serve as much data from the cache as possible, or both. Optimizing both is ideal, but many practical algorithms optimize for one over the other.

There are many replacement strategies to consider when designing a proxy server. The most commonly known cache replacement strategies are least frequently used (LFU) and least recently used (LRU). Podlipnig et al. [2] provided a survey of Web cache replacement strategies. They have done well to not only list well-known strategies, but also categorize the strategies into five groups.

Although both a survey and classification of these strategies are available, there is not a known record of results comparing the majority of the cache replacement

H. ElAarag, *Web Proxy Cache Replacement Strategies*,
SpringerBriefs in Computer Science, DOI: 10.1007/978-1-4471-4893-7_1,
© Hala ElAarag 2013

algorithms. Balamash and Kunz [3] compared cache replacement policies qualitatively rather than quantitatively. Many of the works consulted for this research presented results for different strategies against, at most, three to five other strategies. However, their results cannot be compared effectively because most literature devised their experiments with differences in their implementations, such as the use of auxiliary caching, representation of Web object characteristics. There is also the difference in trace files between experiments and a large range of different sizes used for the cache space. Lastly, different proposals used different criteria on when to cache an object such as ignoring *PHP* files, *cgi-bin* scripts, POST requests, and simply just using all requests presented in a particular trace file.

In spite of the many cache replacement policies proposed in the past years, the most popular Web proxy software, Squid, uses least recently used as its default strategy. We believe that this is because there has not been a comprehensive study presented that compares these strategies quantitatively. As Wong [4] mentions "all policies were purported to perform better than others, creating confusion as to which policy should be used".

In this book, we present a study of cache replacement strategies designed for static Web content, as opposed to dynamic Web content seen in some Web 2.0 applications. Most caching that occurs with dynamic content occurs on the browser side and does not occur from the standpoint of proxy servers. As a result, these strategies have not been considered. We have researched how proxy servers can still improve performance by caching static Web content such as cascading style sheets, java script source files, and most importantly larger files such as images (jpeg, gif, etc.).

This topic is particularly important in wireless ad hoc networks. In such networks, mobile devices act as proxy servers for a group of other mobile devices. However, they have limited storage space. The extensive research on cache replacement policies we provide in this book is crucial for such environments with small cache sizes and limited battery life.

Neural networks have been employed in a number of applications, particularly in the area of pattern recognition. Neural networks are able to learn by experience and hold an internal representation of meaning in data. An appropriately structured neural network will be able to generalize the knowledge acquired from training to data that lies outside the training set. This property makes neural networks useful for solving problems that contain uncertainty or have a problem space which is too large for an exhaustive search. We use neural networks to solve the Web proxy cache replacement problem. A bottom-up approach is justified by the heavy variability in Web traffic which makes general characterization of that traffic difficult. Neural networks are selected for their strength in pattern recognition in noisy data sets. Additionally, they can learn from example by training against a data set, yet are able to generalize beyond the training set. Thus, they are well suited for developing a general replacement strategy from a set of data samples. This approach has the advantage of incorporating subtle traffic pattern information which may be difficult for a human to discern when designing a top-down algorithm.

The rest of the book is organized as follows. Chapter 2 defines Web requests and the characteristics of Web objects and presents some background information about Web proxy servers and Squid. Chapter 3 presents some background information about artificial neural networks. In chap. 4, we present *TWENTY SEVEN* cache replacement strategies we simulated against different performance metrics [5]. To the best our knowledge, this is the most comprehensive quantitative analysis of Web cache replacement strategies. Chapter 5 presents our novel approach to Web proxy cache replacement that uses neural networks for decision making and evaluates its performance and decision structures [6]. We finally present in chap. 6 the implementation of our neural network proxy cache replacement scheme in a real environment, namely in the Squid proxy server [7].

References

1. P. Gill et al., *Youtube traffic characterization: a view from the edge, Proceedings of the 7th ACM SIGCOMM conference on internet measurement* (San Diego, California, USA, 2007), pp. 15–28
2. S. Podlipnig, L. Boszormenyi, A survey of web cache replacement strategies. ACM Comput. Surveys 35(4), 374–398 (2003)
3. A. Balamash, M. Krunz, An overview of web caching replacement algorithms. IEEE Commun. Surveys and Tutorials 6(2), 44–56 (2004)
4. K. Wong, Web cache replacement policies: a pragmatic approach. IEEE Network 20(1), 28–34 (2006)
5. H. ElAarag, S. Romano, A quantitative study of web cache replacement strategies using simulation, simulation: transactions of the society for modeling and simulation international, Sage Publication, Published online before print July 25, 2011. 88(5), 507–541 (2012). doi: 10.1177/0037549711414152
6. W. Cobb, H. ElAarag, Web proxy cache replacement scheme based on back propagation neural network. J. Syst. Software 81(9), 1539–1558 (2008). doi:10.1016/j.jss.2007.10.024
7. S. Romano, H. ElAarag, A neural network proxy cache replacement strategy and its implementation in the squid proxy server. Neural Comput. Appl 20(1), 59–78 (2011). doi:10.1007/s00521-010-0442-0

Chapter 2
Background Information

Keywords Web request · Cacheable request · Web object · Web proxy servers · Squid

It is necessary to have a clear and precise definition on when a Web object is allowed to be cached. A thorough, well-defined definition allows Web cache users to understand what requests they make could potentially be cached, and as well, is necessary for system administrators as a good tool in improving quality of service (QoS) for end users. For this book, a *Web object* is a term used for all possible objects (HTML pages, images, videos, etc.) transferred through the HTTP protocol that can be stored in a proxy cache [1].

2.1 Web Request

A Web request is a reference made through the HTTP protocol to a Web object, primarily referenced by their uniform resource locator (URL). Requests are also identified by the size of the requested Web object from the origin server (at the time the request was made), a HTTP return code, and the time the proxy received the request. We define a *cacheable request* to have the following criteria:

- There must be a defined size, in bytes, for the request, and that size must be less than the total size of the cache and greater than zero.
- The request must be a GET request, and its status code must be one of the following, as set by the HTTP 1.1 protocol [2]: 200, 203, 206, 300, 301, or 410. Table 2.1 shows the status codes and their meanings.

Separate from *cacheable request*, we also ignore any requests with URLs containing "/cgi-bin/" as well as any URLs that are queries (those that contain a question mark in their URL after the last "/").

H. ElAarag, *Web Proxy Cache Replacement Strategies*,
SpringerBriefs in Computer Science, DOI: 10.1007/978-1-4471-4893-7_2,
© Hala ElAarag 2013

Table 2.1 HTTP status code meanings

Code	Meaning
200	Ok
203	Non-authoritative information
206	Partial content
300	Multiple choices
301	Moved permanently
410	Gone (synonymous with deleted)

Once a request is known to be *cacheable* and is received by the proxy, several things will occur in a sequential order. In a basic proxy server model, if a *cache hit* occurs, then the object being referenced is in the cache and the data can be copied and sent to the client. On a *cache miss*, when no object in the cache matches the request, the Web object will be retrieved from the origin server and the *cache placement strategy* decides whether the object will be placed into the cache. If there is not enough room for the new object to be added, then the *cache replacement strategy* is invoked. However, in order to understand how these strategies work, we will define several aspects of objects these strategies will consider.

2.2 Characteristics of Web Objects

Web objects are identified by several different characteristics. Each replacement strategy requires usually a small subset of the characteristics; however, all Web objects must be identified by their URL, since this is the only unique factor. The most important characteristics of Web objects are as follows[1]:

- Recency: information relating to the time the object was last requested.
- Frequency counter: number of requests to the object.
- Size: the size, in bytes, of the Web object.
- Cost: the "cost" incurred for fetching the object from the origin server. Also known as the miss penalty.
- Request value: the benefit gained for storing the object in the cache. This is generally a heuristic-based on other characteristics, since an actual request value of an object cannot be determined without a priori information.
- Expiration time: Also generally a heuristic, defined either by the proxy or by the origin server of when the object will become stale and should be removed or refreshed in the cache. Also known as the time-to-live (TTL).

Most strategies use a combination of these characteristics to make their replacement decisions. The expiration time is the only characteristic mentioned that was not utilized in our simulation and is primarily referenced when dealing with the problem of *cache consistency*, which is out of the scope of this book. The request value is an abstract characteristic, primarily used by *function-based* strategies, and defined by a characteristic function that pursues a total, well-defined ordering of the objects.[1]

2.3 Web Proxy Servers

Web proxy servers are generally configured in one of two basic architectures. In the first configuration, one or more proxy servers are positioned on the network between a Web server or group of Web servers and incoming client traffic from the WAN. The design is aimed at reducing load on the Web server(s). The second architecture is geared toward reducing network congestion. The proxy server(s) is located on the LAN and receives WAN-bound client requests. Figure 2.1 illustrates both architectures. The per-request behavior of a Web proxy server is independent of the choice in architecture. A request for a cached object is served directly. If a request is received for an object not in the cache, the proxy requests the object from the Web server, which potentially caches the object and then serves the object to the client. This process is shown in Fig. 2.2.

Web proxy caching is a paging problem. Strategies applied to other paging problems, such as main memory management, have been adapted to address Web proxy caching. Web proxy caching has two main factors that must be addressed: cache replacement and cache consistency. Cache replacement refers to deciding what should be removed from the cache to make room for new data. Cache consistency refers to ensuring that items in the cache are still the same as items on the original server. This book will address the former.

2.4 Squid

Squid [3] is an open source proxy cache project now maintained by volunteers, originally supported through an NSF grant, and now fueled purely by donations. Squid currently supports HTTP 1.0 protocol and is almost HTTP 1.1 compliant. One difference between HTTP 1.0 and 1.1 protocols is the cacheable request definition. For instance, partial requests (return code 206) are not allowed to be cached in Squid, as opposed to HTTP 1.1 compliant software, which is allowed to be cached. Through Squid's configuration files and easy compilation steps, one can control almost any aspect of the cache including the replacement strategy and how the proxy logs requests, such as keeping a log of the requests that Squid automatically saves to the hard disk. In the early 1990s, the Squid project came about

---

[1] Essentially, any characteristic could be the request value, if the algorithm makes its decision based on one variable that has a total, well-defined ordering.

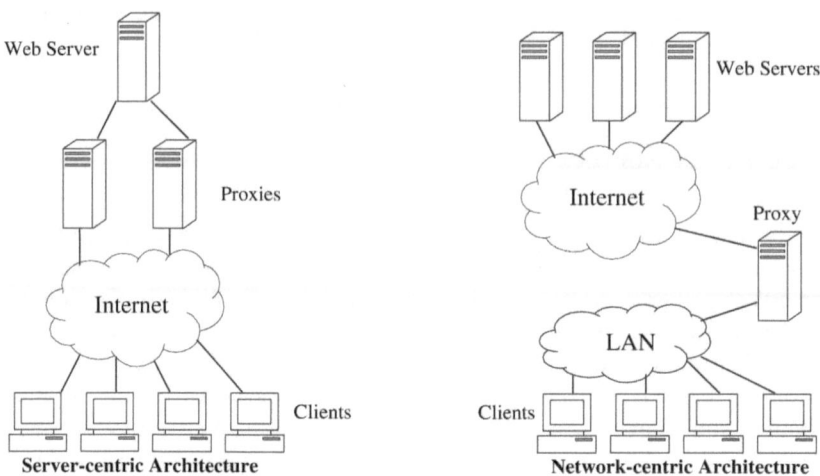

Fig. 2.1 Web proxy cache architectures

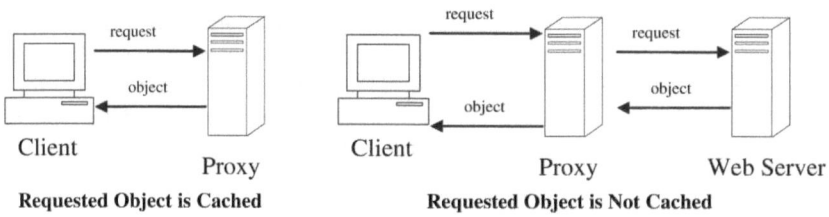

Fig. 2.2 Web proxy cache request sequence

from a fork of the Harvest Cache Daemon. The other fork existing today is NetApp's NetCache [3], which is a proprietary software package.

Originally, the NSF funded Squid in order to promote research in the 1990s before the conception of broadband, DSL, and other technologies that lead to a huge increase in bandwidth. As far as many businesses and researchers were concerned, the Web caching problem was essentially deemed "solved" in the late 1990s and early part of this decade [1]. Most of these strategies were simple due to the lack of CPU power, available RAM, and especially available storage. In fact, it was rare to see a proxy server that had more than 2 gigabytes of space devoted to the cache. Today, this amount of disk space is trivial.

However, the decrease in costs for bandwidth, increase in CPU power, greater storage capacities, and higher demand for download speed have led to bandwidth problems again especially for Web publishers who host major Web sites. Increase in use of dynamic pages as well is leading to yet another strain in the bandwidth provided by today's broadband/WAN technologies. These new dilemmas have led many companies, businesses, and even Internet service providers (ISPs) to turn to research in caching. However, many strategies authored in the late 1990s and early part of this decade are failing in being able to dynamically adapt to request streams and the constantly changing environment that the Internet has now become.

References

1. S. Podlipnig, L. Boszormenyi, A survey of web cache replacement strategies. ACM Comput. Surveys **35**(4), 374–398 (2003)
2. Hypertext transfer protocol–HTTP/1.1 [online document] [cited Aug. 14, 2007] available. WWW: http://www.w3.org/Protocols/rfc2616/rfc2616.html
3. What is squid?, available at http://www.squid-cache.org/Intro/

Chapter 3
Neural Networks

Keywords Neural network · Feed-forward multi-layer perceptrons · Firing rule · Squashing function · Supervised learning · Objective function · Backpropagation

Neural networks are comprised of many interconnected simple processing units (neurons), which (when combined) are able to approximate functions based on data sets [1]. Neural networks typically mimic biologic neurons by using a set of weights, one for each connection, which is similar to the exciting and inhibiting properties of actual neurons [1–4]. By adjusting these weights such that the network is able to provide correct outputs for most of (ideally all of) the inputs, the network is said to gain knowledge about the problem. This is particularly useful for problems where a definite and/or optimal algorithm is unknown. Neural networks are also valuable for developing heuristics for problems where the data set is too large for a comprehensive search [2].

A neuron with an associated weight for each connection is known as a McCulloch and Pitts (MCP) neuron [1]. A neural network comprised of MCP neurons is considerably more powerful than a neural network with unweighted neurons. The weights allow the network to develop its own representation of knowledge [2]. The output of each neuron is determined by applying a function to the sum of every output multiplied by the weight of the associated connection [1–5]. The MCP model does not suggest a specific rule for the translating neuron input to output, so one must be chosen according to the properties of the problem the network is designed to solve.

H. ElAarag, *Web Proxy Cache Replacement Strategies*,
SpringerBriefs in Computer Science, DOI: 10.1007/978-1-4471-4893-7_3,
© Hala ElAarag 2013

3.1 Firing Rule/Squashing Function

The firing rule determines whether or not the neuron will "fire" based on the inputs. Neuron firing rules are generally linear (proportional output), threshold (binary output), or sigmoid (nonlinear proportional output) [1]. Although "firing" is a simple on or off for threshold networks, it is more typically used to mean a rule for determining the amount of output. Neural networks that use nonlinear proportional output sometimes refer to the firing rule as the squashing function because they are typically chosen to constrain extreme positive and negative values. The terms firing rule, squashing function, and activation function are used interchangeably. Common squashing functions include the sigmoid, tanh, and step functions [5]. The sigmoid and tanh functions are approximately linear close to zero but quickly saturate for larger positive or negative numbers. The sigmoid function,

$$f(u) = \frac{1}{1 + e^{-u}} \tag{3.1}$$

is 0.5 for $u = 0$ and is bounded by 0 and 1. The tanh function,

$$f(u) = \frac{e^u - e^{-u}}{e^u + e^{-u}} \tag{3.2}$$

is 0 for $u = 0$ and is bounded by -1 and 1. Sigmoid and tanh functions both have derivatives which are easy to calculate given the output. For the sigmoid function, the derivative is

$$f'(u) = f(u)(1 - f(u)), \tag{3.3}$$

and for tanh, the derivative is

$$f'(u) = 1 - f^2(u) \tag{3.4}$$

3.2 Multi-Layer Perceptrons

All neural networks have a layer of inputs and a layer of outputs. Neural networks which also feature one or more additional "hidden" layers are called multi-layer perceptrons (MLP) [1, 5]. In this research, we employ a feed-forward network.

Fig. 3.1 MLP neural network with two input nodes, two hidden layers with three nodes each, and one output node

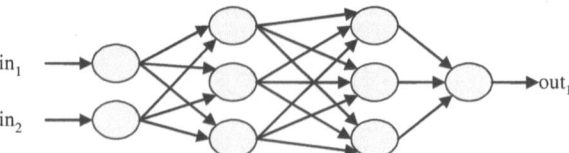

Feed-forward networks are fully connected, meaning all of the neurons in a given layer, proceeding from input to output, are connected to each neuron in the next layer. Figure 3.1 shows one possible MLP configuration with the arrows indicating the direction of signal propagation.

The output y_i of node i is $f(a_i)$, where f is the activation function and a_i is the activity on node i. The activity is

$$a_i = \sum_{j<i} w_{ij} y_j, \qquad (3.5)$$

where wij is the weight of the connection to node i from node j. The name is derived from the fact that signals always proceed forward (from input to output) in the network [1, 3, 5]. Feedback networks also exist, but are more complicated and less intuitive than feed-forward networks. In a feedback network, neurons may be connected to other neurons in the same layer, a previous layer, or even to itself. These networks, unlike feed-forward networks, fluctuate upon receiving new input until reaching an equilibrium point [1]. A feed-forward MLP with two hidden layers is able to classify regions of any shape [5, 6] and approximate any continuous bounded function [5, 7].

3.3 Supervised Learning

The MLP model described earlier requires the weights to be tuned to the specific problem the network is designed to address. Supervised learning is one method of determining the proper weights. The MLP is trained on inputs where the corresponding target output is known. The weights are then adjusted according to the correctness of the produced output. This process is repeated until the network is able to provide the correct output for each of the training inputs or until a stopping condition is satisfied [1–5]. Since the MLP approximates a function that matches the training data, this approach aims to achieve weights that allow the network to generalize to input/output combinations that are not included in the training set. In practical applications, the MLP needs two methods: one to measure how closely a training output matches the target output and a second to adjust the weights such that the error level is reduced [1, 5].

3.4 Objective Function

The objective function, also called the error function, is used to quantify the level of correctness of training output. According to [5], the sum of squared errors is the most commonly used objective function. However, all objective functions make some assumptions about the distribution of errors and perform accordingly. Some

applications require objective functions that lack the benefit of easy differentia-
bility and/or independence found in the most common error functions [5]. The sum
of squared errors (SSE) is given by:

$$E_{SSE} = \frac{1}{2} \sum_p \sum_o (t_o - y_o)^2 \tag{3.6}$$

where o is indexed over the output nodes, p is indexed over the training patterns, t_o
is the target output, and y_o is the actual output. The mean sum of squared error
function normalizes SSE for the number of training patterns and is given by:

$$E_{MSE} = \frac{1}{P} E_{SSE}, \tag{3.7}$$

where P is the number of training patterns. SSE and MSE both assume a Gaussian
error distribution. For classification problems, the cross-entropy error function

$$E_{CE} = - \sum_p \sum_o t_{po} \ln(y_{po}) + (1 - t_{po}) \ln(1 - y_{po}), \tag{3.8}$$

where $t \in \{0, 1\}$. The cross-entropy error function assumes a binomial distribution, and outputs and targets are interpreted as a probability or confidence level
that the pattern belongs to a certain class.

3.5 Backpropagation

Backpropagation is the most commonly used method of adjusting the weights in a
MLP. It calculates the partial derivative of the error with respect to each weight by
calculating the rate of change in the error as the activity for each unit changes. The
delta values δ_i are first calculated for the output layer directly based on the target
and actual outputs. For *SSE*, this is

$$\delta_i = f_i'(t_i - y_i) \tag{3.9}$$

It is not necessary, fortunately, to calculate the derivative of the cross-entropy
error function. If the cross-entropy error function is used with sigmoid units, then
δ_i for output nodes is simply

$$\delta_i = t_i - y_i \tag{3.10}$$

The same calculations are then performed for each hidden layer based on
information from the layer "in front" of that layer. Once the error derivative of the
weights is known, they can be adjusted to reduce the error. Backpropagation is so
named because the error derivatives are calculated in the opposite direction of
signal propagation. The delta value δ_i of node i for hidden nodes is calculated as
follows:

$$\delta_i = f_i' \sum_{k > i} w_{ki} \delta_k \,, \tag{3.11}$$

where $i < k$. This process is repeated until the error is less than a threshold determined by the application of the network [1–5].

Reed and Marks [5] point out that backpropagation actually refers to both the derivative calculation and a weight change algorithm. The basic weight update algorithm changes each weight by negative, the derivative of the error with respect to the weights multiplied by a small constant η known as the learning rate (LR), as shown in Eq. 3.12.

$$\Delta w_{ij} = \eta \frac{\partial E}{\partial w_{ij}} \tag{3.12}$$

Momentum is a common modification to the weight update algorithm which involves adding a fraction of the previous weight change to the current weight change [5]. The backpropagation weight update amount with momentum is

$$\Delta w_{ij}(t) = \eta \frac{\partial E}{\partial w_{ij}}(t) + \alpha \Delta w_{ij}(t - 1), \tag{3.13}$$

where $0 \leq \alpha < 1$ is the momentum rate (MR). Momentum is useful for coasting out of a poor local minima in the error surface and traversing flat areas quickly [5].

Two common variations of this algorithm are batch-mode and online learning. Batch-mode learning runs all patterns in a training set. The error derivative with respect to the weight for each pattern is summed to obtain the total error derivative with respect to the weights. All weights are then adjusted accordingly. Online training, on the other hand, runs a pattern at random from the training set. The weights are updated after each single pattern using the error derivative with respect to the weights for the current training pattern [5].

References

1. C. Stergiou, D. Siganos, Neural Networks, [Online document] [cited Sept. 9, 2005] Available WWW: http://www.doc.ic.ac.uk/~nd/surprise_96/journal/vol4/cs11/report.html
2. L. Fu, Knowledge discovery based on neural networks. Commun. ACM. Arch **42**(11), 47–50 (1999)
3. P P. Van der Smagt, A comparative study of neural network algorithms applied to optical character recognition, in *Proceedings of the third international conference on industrial and engineering applications of artificial intelligence and expert systems* vol. 2 (ACM Press, New York, 1990), pp. 1037–1044
4. B. Dasgupta, H.T. Siegelmann, E. Sontag, On a learnability question associated to neural networks with continuous activations, *Annual Workshop on Computational Learning Theory*, pp. 47–56, 1994
5. R.D. Reed, R.J. Marks II, *Neural Smithing: Supervised Learning in Feedforward Artificial Neural Networks* (The MIT Press, Cambridge, MA, 1999)

6. R. P. Lippmann, An introduction to computing with neural nets, *ASSP Magazine*, pp. 4–22, April 1987
7. A. Lapedes, R. Farber, *"How Neural Nets Work"*, *in Neural Information Processing Systems* (American Institute of Physics, New York, 1988) pp. 442–456

Chapter 4
A Quantitative Study of Web Cache Replacement Strategies Using Simulation

Keywords Web proxies · Proxy caching · Cache replacement algorithm · Simulation · Performance evaluation · Recency-based strategies · Frequency-based strategies · Function-based strategies · Hit rate · Byte-hit rate · Removal rate · Trace file · IRCache

4.1 Introduction

The Web has become the most important source of information and communication for the world. Proxy servers are used to cache objects with the goals of decreasing network traffic, reducing user perceived lag and loads on origin servers. Despite that some Web 2.0 applications have dynamic objects, most of the Web traffic has static content with file types such as cascading style sheets, javascript files, images. The cache replacement strategies implemented in Squid, a widely used proxy cache software, are no longer considered "good enough" today. Squid's default strategy is least recently used (LRU). While this is a simple approach, it does not necessarily achieve the targeted goals. In this chapter, we present the simulation of *twenty-seven* proxy cache replacement strategies and analyze them against several important performance measures. Hit rate and byte-hit rate are the most commonly used performance metrics in the literature. Hit rate is an indication of user perceived lag, while byte-hit rate is an indication of the amount of network traffic. We also introduce a new performance metric, the object removal rate, which is an indication of CPU usage and disk access at the proxy server. This metric is particularly important for busy cache servers or servers with lower processing power. Our study provides valuable insights for both industry and academia. They are especially important for Web proxy cache system administrators, particularly in wireless ad hoc networks as the cache on mobile devices is relatively small.

H. ElAarag, *Web Proxy Cache Replacement Strategies*,
SpringerBriefs in Computer Science, DOI: 10.1007/978-1-4471-4893-7_4,
© Hala ElAarag 2013

Table 4.1 Cache replacement categories

Category	Rationale	Replacement policies
Recency based	Derived from a property known as temporal locality, the measure of how likely an object is to appear again in a request stream after being requested within a time span [29]	LRU, LRU-Threshold [3], Pitkow/ Reckers strategy [4], SIZE [5], LOG2-SIZE [1], LRU-Min [3], Value-Aging [6], HLRU [8] and Pyramidal Selection Scheme (PSS) [9]
Frequency based	Derived from an object's popularity where those that are most popular should be cached [1, 2].	LFU, LFU-Aging [10], LFU-DA [10] and α-Aging [6], LFU* [30]
Frequency/ recency based	Attempt to combine both spatial and temporal locality together maintaining their characteristics of the previous two classes.	Segmented LRU (SLRU) [10], Generational replacement [11], LRU* [12], HYPER-G [5], Cubic Selection Scheme (CSS) [13], and LRU-SP [14]
Function based	Use a general characteristic function to define a request value for objects.	Greedy-Dual (GD)-Size [15], GDSF [17], GD* [16], Taylor series prediction (TSP) [18], MIX [19], M-Metric [20], LNC-R-W3 [21], and LUV [22]

The rest of the chapter is structured as follows. We describe the cache replacement categorization, rationale, and example policies in Sect. 4.2. Section 4.3 discusses our simulation and certain data structures used for the algorithms. We define the metrics used to measure the performance of each strategy and also propose a new metric in Sect. 4.4. Section 4.5 presents the results and observations of our simulation. The conclusion of this chapter is presented in Sect. 4.6.

4.2 Replacement Strategies

Cache replacement strategies can be categorized into five groups: frequency based, recency based, frequency/recency based, function based, and randomized [1]. Wong [2] also categorizes cache replacement strategies into five groups, but instead of recency/frequency category, a size category is suggested. We adopt the classification of Podlipnig [1] in this chapter.

The first two groups, *recency* and *frequency*, are based mainly on least recently used and least frequently used (LFU), respectively. *Frequency/recency* strategies incorporate a mixture of an object's recency and frequency information together along with other characteristics to refine LRU and LFU. *Function-based* strategies have some defined method that accepts certain predefined parameters defining a request value to order the objects in the cache. The last group, *random*, essentially picks an object in a non-deterministic method. Due to strategies' inconsistent nature of the last category, we decided not to include any strategies that had a non-determinate replacement strategy. Table 4.1 presents the replacement categories, their rationale, and some example of available replacement policies.

4.3 Simulation Details

This section provides the details for our simulation and how some of the strategies were implemented. We also describe other Web cache strategies and components we used that were not part of our research, but integral to building a functional Web cache.

4.3.1 Web Cache Components

As discussed in Chap. 2, there are several decisions that must be made during the life span of a Web request. The first decision is to decide whether the current request is cacheable. Once a request is known to be cacheable, it is searched among the objects in the cache and determined whether it already exists or not. If the object exists, it must be determined whether the data in the cache have passed its expiration time. If the expiration time is up or the object was not in the cache, the object is retrieved from the origin server, then the Web object's information (recency, frequency counters, request value, etc.) is updated, and the next request is served.

Once an object is retrieved from the origin server, a cache *placement* strategy is invoked, deciding whether the cache will accept the object or not before it is sent to the client. If not enough space exists in the cache, the cache *replacement* strategy is invoked.

Most proxy caches also use two limits to their space available in the cache and make sure the cache can respond well in case of sudden increases in the incoming number of requests. They set what are known as two watermarks. One is called a *low watermark* and is often symbolized by *L*; the other is known as the *high watermark* and is symbolized as *H*. If the current space occupied by the cache exceeds *H*, then the replacement strategy, also known as the victim selection process, is invoked until the space is less than or equal to *L*. Typically, *L* is set to 60–75 % of the cache's total space and *H* set to 90–95 % of the total cache space.

However, in the case of our simulation, we ignored the watermark process, to see how much strain the Web cache could take as well as how well the replacement strategies worked when invoked under necessary conditions (no space being left) as opposed to being invoked prior to the cache being full.

In order to create these conditions, we also had to ignore the expiration process. Typically, either the object's TTL[1] is used or a heuristic is generated based on the

---

[1] A web object's Time-To-Live, or amount of time till the object is considered "expired".

file's size, URL, etc. This was not the focus of our research, and since the trace files we utilized provided no information on the TTL of the object at the time the traces were recorded, it was out of our scope to investigate known expiration policies. Last, but not least, our cache placement was a simple strategy. All objects whose requests were deemed cacheable were immediately intended to be cached.

Some literature make a distinction in their cache placement strategy, admitting only those objects which will add an overall *benefit* to the cache so in the case that the replacement strategy must be invoked the *benefit* of the object being added must outweigh the *benefit* of those objects being removed from the cache.

In essence, this treats the *caching problem* as the famous *knapsack problem*, which is an excellent comparison. However, most definitions are ambiguous as to what the benefit is measured by. Also, the benefit should be dynamic and decreasing due to objects' expiration times. If expiration time is not a factor, then the benefit would need to consider recency information. But in considering recency information, we also have to consider how recently the last request to the object being considered occurred, leading to more space overhead for objects not in our cache, which adds even more complexity to the entire process.

Without considering recency, expiration, or any factor involving durations of time, then the cache will suffer a similar pollution to what LFU tends to create, which is the caching of only those objects deemed to be overall beneficial. This is exactly the outcome one would expect in terms of the *knapsack* problem; but in terms of the *caching* problem, this is what we wish to avoid. Thus, we decided against considering more complex placement procedures due to no previous method to calculate *benefit* and to focus on the replacement process.

4.3.2 Simulation Architecture

Our simulator was built as a discrete event simulator where each request was treated as a discrete event. The simulation clock was advanced forward by the amount of time that passed from request to request so that the time in the simulation was artificially equivalent to the time that the request in the trace took place at. Trace files were parsed and cleansed prior to the simulation. We identified requests referring to the same URI and gave all unique URI's a specific unique identification number. Figure 4.1 illustrates the request life cycle and how simulation statistics are recorded.

4.3.3 Details of Implemented Strategies

Table 4.2 contains commonly used variables and their descriptions. If a strategy uses a variable not defined in the table, then it will be defined in their corresponding implementation detail. Any use of the logarithmic function, symbolized as *log*, is assumed to be of base 2, unless otherwise specified.

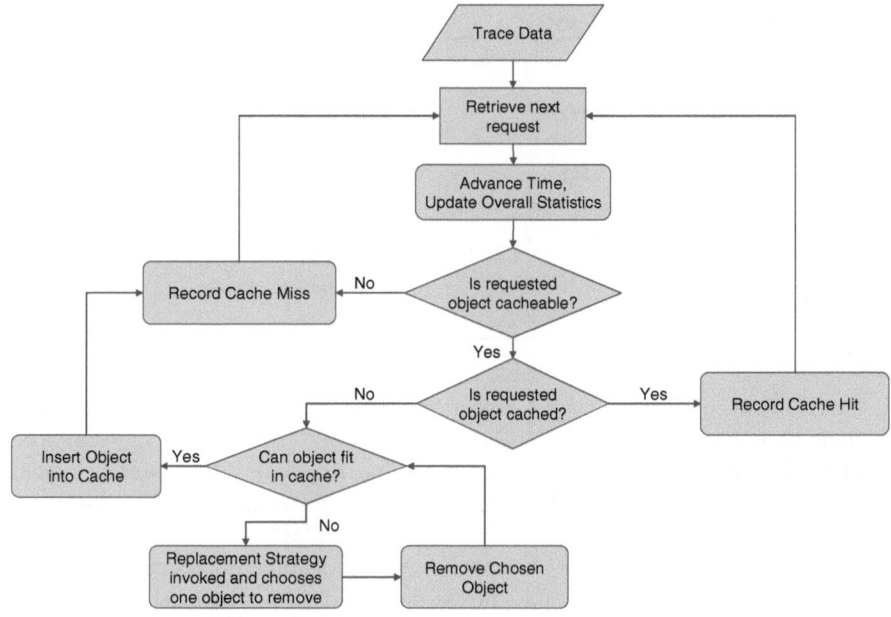

Fig. 4.1 Simulated request life cycle

Note that some strategies require use of an auxiliary cache. An auxiliary cache holds information about all Web objects that have been seen by the proxy cache. Without this stored information, particular strategies tend to produce less than optimal results as explained later.

4.3.3.1 Implementation of Recency-Based Strategies

This set of strategies use recency information as a significant part of their victim selection process. Recency-based strategies are typically straight forward to implement taking advantage of queues and linked lists.

1. **LRU**: One of the most commonly used strategies in many areas of data management. This algorithm removes the least recently used (referenced) object, or in other terms, the object with the largest ΔT_i. A simple linked list (queue) allows this algorithm to be efficiently implemented and is referred as a LRU list.
2. **LRU-Threshold** [3]: Just like LRU, except an object is not permitted into the cache if its size, S_i, exceeds a given threshold.
3. **Pitkow/Reckers strategy** [4]: Objects that are most recently referenced within the same day are differentiated by size, choosing the largest first. Object references not in the same period are sorted by LRU. This strategy can be extended by varying the period of which objects are differentiated by their size (such as an h, 2 days, 1 week.).

Table 4.2 Characteristic symbols

Variable	Description
S_i	Size of an object i
T_i	Time object i was last requested
ΔT_i	Time since object i was last request
F_i	Frequency counter of object i
ΔF_i	Number of references to occur since last time object i was referenced
l_i	Access latency for object i
C_i	Cost of object i
R_i	Request value of object i
M	Size of the cache

4. **SIZE** [5]: Removes the largest object first. If objects are of the same size, then their tie is broken by LRU.
5. **LOG2-SIZE** [1]: Sorts objects by their $floor[log(S_i)]$, differentiating objects with the same value by LRU. This strategy tends to invoke LRU more often between similar-sized objects as compared to SIZE.
6. **LRU-Min** [3]: This strategy attempts to remove as little documents as possible while using LRU. Let T be the current threshold, L_o be the least recently used object (tail of a LRU list), and L an object in the list. Then LRU-Min follows as so:

   (a) Set T to S_i of the object being admitted to the cache.
   (b) Set L to L_o.
   (c) If L is greater than or equal to T, then remove L. If it is not, set L to the next LRU object in the list and repeat this step again until there is enough space or the end of the list is reached.
   (d) If the end of the list is reached, then divide T by 2 and repeat the process from step 2.

7. **Value-Aging** [6]: Defines a characteristic function based on the time of a new request to object i and removes the smallest value, R_i. Letting C_t be the current time, R_i is initialized to:

$$R_i = C_t \times \sqrt{\frac{C_t}{2}} \qquad (4.1)$$

At each request, R_i is updated to:

$$R_i = C_t \times \sqrt{\frac{C_t - T_i}{2}} \qquad (4.2)$$

8. **HLRU** [7]: Standing for history LRU, this uses a sliding window of h request times for objects. This algorithm is fairly complicated compared with most algorithms in this set, requiring additional information to be held for each object, even after the object has been removed from the cache. It is entirely

possible to implement the algorithm without an auxiliary cache, but we found the results to be far less than optimal. The author of the algorithm also defined the algorithm with an auxiliary cache in mind. The *hist* value is defined for an object x with n indexed request times, t, where t_i is equivalent to the ith request time of object x.

$$\text{hist}(x, h) = \begin{cases} t_{n-h} & n \geq h \\ 0 & n < h \end{cases} \tag{4.3}$$

HLRU chooses the object with the maximum *hist* value. If multiple objects have *hist* values of 0, then they are sorted based on LRU.

9. **Pyramidal Selection Scheme (PSS)** [8]: This classification makes what is known as a "pyramidal" hierarchy of classes based on their size. Objects of a class j have sizes ranging from 2^{j-1} to 2^{j-1}. Inversely, an object i belongs to the class $j = floor[log(S_i)]$. There are $N = ceil [log(M + 1)]$ classes. Each class is managed by its own LRU list. To select the next victim during the replacement process, the recently used objects of each class are compared based on their value, $S_i \times \Delta F_i$. In Sect. 4.4, we will demonstrate an efficient way to calculate ΔF_i in $O(1)$ time without keeping record of the request stream.

4.3.3.2 Implementation of Frequency-Based Strategies

Obviously, this category is tied strongly to the frequency/access counts of Web objects. Unlike recency-based strategies, these simple algorithms require complex data structures, such as binary heaps (also known as priority queues) to help decrease the time overhead in making their decisions. Some strategies, such as SIZE and HLRU, also take advantage of binary heaps. However, we considered this to be a detail oddity compared with most recency-based strategies.

Most of these algorithms are an extension of the common algorithm LFU. There are two ways to implement these algorithms, one requiring use of an auxiliary cache and the other not. Comparatively, most recency-based strategies only need to keep track of the most *recent* values seen by the proxy cache, simplifying the record of a Web object's data to the time it is in the cache even if it is removed and added repeatedly. However, frequency counts do not pertain only to the life span of a particular object in the cache, but can also be persistent across multiple lifetimes of the object. The persistent recording of data for an object's frequency counts is known as *perfect LFU*, which inevitably requires more space overhead. The tracking of data while the object is only in the cache is known as *in-Cache LFU*.

In either *perfect* or *in-cache* implementations, the cache can suffer *cache pollution*, objects with high-frequency counts that persist in the cache despite no longer being popular. Objects accumulating high popularity in many bursts over long periods of time create a problem with *perfect LFU*. However, *in-cache* suffers from missing the objects that slowly accumulate popularity over a long period, caching only those that happen to accumulate high popularity in the short run.

There are flaws with both implementations; some in this section and the next will seek to break those down.

Since there is space overhead with *perfect LFU*, we will assume the *in-cache* variants of these algorithms.

10. **LFU**: The base algorithm of this class removes the least frequently used object (or object with the smallest frequency counter).
11. **LFU-Aging** [9]: This strategy attempts to remove the problem of cache pollution due to objects that become popular in a short time period. To avoid it, this strategy introduces an aging factor. When the average of all the frequency counters in the cache exceeds a given average frequency threshold, then all frequency counts are divided by 2 (with a minimum of 1 for F_i). There is also a maximum threshold set that no frequency counter is allowed to exceed.
12. **LFU-DA** [9]: Since the performance of LFU-Aging requires the right threshold and maximum frequency, LFU-DA tries to remove this problem. Upon a request to object i, its value, K_i, is calculated as:

$$K_i = F_i + L, \tag{4.4}$$

where L is a dynamic aging factor. Initially L is set to 0, but upon the removal of an object i, L is set to K_i. This strategy removes the object with the smallest K_i value.
13. **α-Aging** [6]: It is a periodic aging method that can use varying periods and a range, [0, 1], for its aging factor, α. Each object in this strategy uses a value, K, which is incremented by 1 each cache hit, much like a frequency counter. At the end of each period, an aging factor is applied to each object:

$$K_{\text{new}} = \alpha \times K, 0 \leq \alpha \leq 1 \tag{4.5}$$

Changing α from 0 to 1, one can obtain a spectrum of algorithms ranging from LRU ($\alpha = 0$) to LFU ($\alpha = 1$). Of course, this is only true if LRU is used as a tiebreaker [1].

4.3.3.3 Implementation of Frequency/Recency-Based Strategies

These strategies tend to be fairly complex in their structure and procedures.

14. **Segmented LRU (SLRU)** [10]: This strategy partitions the cache into a two-tier system. One segment is known as the *unprotected* segment and the other, the *protected* segment. The strategy requires space set aside for the protected segment. Objects that belong to this segment cannot be removed from the cache once added. Both segments are managed by the LRU replacement strategy. When an object is added to the cache, it is added to the unprotected segment, removing only objects from the unprotected space to make room for it. There is an implicit size threshold for objects, where the minimum object

size allowed to be cached is *min{size of the protected segment, M—size of protected segment}*. Upon a cache hit of an object, it is moved to the front of the protected segment. If the object is in the unprotected segment and there is not enough room in the protected segment, the LRU strategy is applied till there is enough room for the object to be moved into it. Objects removed from the protected segment are moved to the head of the unprotected segment.

15. **Generational Replacement**: [11]: This strategy uses n $(n > 1)$ LRU lists. Each list is indexed, 1, 2 … n. Upon being added to the cache, an object is added to the head of list (a). Upon a cache hit, an object belonging to list i is moved to the head of list $i + 1$, unless $i = n$, and then, the object is moved to the head of list n. Victim selection begins at the end of list 1 and moves to the next consecutive list only when preceding lists have been depleted.

16. **LRU*** [12]: This method combines a LRU list and what is known as a "request" [1] counter. When an object enters the cache, its request counter is set to 1 and it is added to the front of the list. On a cache hit, its request counter is incremented by 1 and also moved to the front of the list. During victim selection, the request counter of the least recently used object (the tail of the list) is checked. If it is zero, the object is removed from the list; if it is not zero, its request counter is decremented by 1 and moved to the front of the list, and the same process is applied until the new object can be added.

17. **HYPER-G** [5]: This strategy combines LRU, LFU, and SIZE. At first, the least frequently used object is chosen. If there is more than one object with the same frequency value, the cache chooses the least recently used among them. If this still does not give a unique object to replace, the largest object is chosen. These next two strategies are extensions of the recency-based PSS strategy mentioned in Sect. 4.3.1.

18. **Cubic Selection Scheme (CSS)** [13]: As the name implies, CSS uses a cube-like structure to select its victims. Like PSS, CSS assigns objects to classes, except rather than being indexed only by size; CSS indexes classes by size and frequency counts. Each class, like PSS, is a LRU list. Objects in a class (j, k) have sizes and frequencies ranging from $2^{(j, k-1)}$ to $2^{(j, k)-1}$. Inversely, an object i belongs to class $(j, k) = (floor[log\ S_i], floor[log\ F_i])$. The width, which is the largest value of j, is the same as in PSS, since it is based on cache size. But, in order to limit space overhead, there must also be a maximum frequency, *MaxF*, set to limit the height of the cube. Thus, the height of the cube is *floor* $[log\ MaxF] + 1$. CSS uses a complicated procedure to select its victims, considering the diagonals of the cube and the LRU objects in each list. There is also an "aging mechanism" applied based on the *MaxF* set for the cube.

19. **LRU-SP** [14]: Like PSS, this class utilizes classes managed by LRU and has the same number of classes as PSS, each managed by LRU. However, this class accounts for frequency counts as well. An object i is assigned to class $j = floor[log(Si/F_i + 1)]$. Essentially, as an object is requested more

frequently, it decreases the class it is in. When a victim is to be selected, all the LRU objects of each list are compared based on the value $(\Delta T_i \times S_i)/F_i$.

4.3.3.4 Implementation of Function-Based Strategies

These functions use a general characteristic function to define a request value for objects. Most of these algorithms are straight forward requiring a binary heap to sort objects; however, several can become quite time consuming once the recency variable, ΔT_i, has been introduced, requiring a resorting/recalculation of objects when the cache replacement strategy must be invoked. If it is not stated, then we assume that the strategy always picks the object with the smallest request value.

20. **Greedy-Dual (GD)-Size** [15]: Defines a request value, R_i, for the object which is recalculated upon insertion of on a cache hit:

$$R_i = \frac{C_i}{S_i} + L \qquad (4.6)$$

L is an aging factor like in LFU-DA described in Sect. 4.3.2 and initialized to zero. Whenever an object is removed, L is set to that removed object's R_i value. R_i is calculated upon an object request as it is placed in the cache. The factor, C_i/S_i, is known as the "normalized cost." The normalized cost is meant to describe a proportion of an object's request cost to its size as opposed to a typical Landlord algorithm, which assumes uniform size [16].

21. **GDSF** [17]: As an extension of GD-Size, this uses the frequency information as well to define a value. The request value is defined as:

$$R_i = \frac{F_i \times C_i}{S_i} + L \qquad (4.7)$$

L is an aging factor used exactly like in GD-Size.

22. **GD*** [16]: As an extension of *GDSF*, this method uses a predetermined calculation of temporal locality signified in a variable, β, known as the reference correlation. Reference correlation is measured by the distribution of reference interarrivals for equally popular objects [1]. The variable is meant to be figured optimally by using trace files. However, the authors of the algorithm found the optimal variable to be 1.66, which seemed to produce the optimal metrics for us as well. The request value is calculated as:

$$R_i = \left(\frac{F_i \times C_i}{S_i}\right)^{1/\beta} + L \qquad (4.8)$$

L is an aging factor used exactly like in GD-Size.

23. **Taylor Series Prediction (TSP)** [18]: TSP calculates the request value as follows:

$$R_i = \frac{F_i \times C_i}{S_i \times T_t} \tag{4.9}$$

T_T is the "temporal acceleration" of an object with respect to the current time and its last and next to last request times. $T_T = t_p - t_c$, where t_p is the predicted time for the next request and t_c, the current time. The predicted time is solved using a second-order Taylor series. It should be noted that the variable T_T is similar in concept to ΔT_i, which means it must be recalculated before the cache replacement process begins.

24. **MIX** [19]: A heavily parameterized strategy, MIX, is an all-around algorithm which can be tuned for any metric. There are four parameters, referenced as $r_i\{i \mid 1, 2, 3, 4\}$. The request value is calculated as follows:

$$R_i = \frac{l_i^{r1} \times F_i^{r2}}{S_i^{r3} \times \Delta T_i^{r4}} \tag{4.10}$$

According to Podlipnig [1], the authors of the algorithm used $r_1 = 0.1$ and $r_{\{2,3,4\}} = 1$. There are no defined ranges, but adjusting the parameters greatly adjusts the factors making the algorithm fairly robust. The only exception is that no aging method is applied in this strategy, but an extension could introduce an aging factor much like GD-Size, etc.

25. **M-Metric** [20]: This strategy takes three parameters: f, s, and t. With these in mind, it defines the request value as:

$$R_i = F_i^f \times S_i^s \times \Delta T_i^t \tag{4.11}$$

f should be positive as to give weight to popular objects. A positive s value will give higher weight to larger objects, while a negative value will give higher weight to smaller objects; t reflects how much recency is taken into account. A positive value gives weight to older objects, while a negative value will result in younger objects taking precedence over older. Based on the parameter values, this algorithm will decide exactly like LRU ($f = 0$, $s = 0$, $t < 0$), LFU ($f > 0$, $s = 0$, $t = 0$), and SIZE ($f = 0$, $s < 0$, $t = 0$).

26. **LNC-R-W3** [21]: This method sets a parameter b, which is meant to change the importance of object sizes like in M-Metric. There is also a parameter K, which designates the past K request times to keep track of. Letting t be the current time and t_k be the oldest request time in the sliding window of K requests for an object i, f_i is set as:

$$f_i = \frac{K}{((t_c - t_k) \times S_i^b)} \tag{4.12}$$

f_i is then used to calculate the request value as shown in Eq. 4.13.

$$R_i = \frac{f_i \times l_i}{S_i} \tag{4.13}$$

27. **LUV** [22]: Like the other function-based strategies, least unified value (LUV) also defines a request value for each object i..

$$R_i = W(i) \times p(i) \tag{4.14}$$

$$W(i) = \frac{C_i}{S_i} \tag{4.15}$$

$W(i)$ is known as the normalized, or relative, cost to fetch the object from its origin server. The other factor in the request value represents the "probability" that an object i will be referenced again. $p(i)$ is defined as: .

$$p(i) = \sum_{k=1}^{F_i} H(t_c - t_k) \tag{4.16}$$

$$H(x) = \left(\frac{1}{2}\right)^{\lambda x}, (0 \le \lambda \le 1), \tag{4.17}$$

where t_c is the current time and t_k is the reference time in a sliding window of F_i request times. It should also be noted that $F(x)$ can be any function, so long as the function is decreasing. We have only provided the function suggested by Bahn et al. [22] and used in our simulations.

4.3.4 Other Implementation Details

The implementation language we decided to use was Java SDK 6.0. Though concerned with speed, Java performed well on the simulation machine in Ubuntu 7.04 with Intel Core 2 Duo E6600 (2.4 GHz) and 2 GB of RAM. We were able to parallelize the simulations, being able to take advantage of the dual core processor. The only limitations we encountered were memory intensive algorithms, which require the use of an auxiliary cache in order to make their decisions. Our solution to the problem was to flag those algorithms which were memory intensive and run only one memory intensive algorithm at a time (memory intensive algorithms could run with other algorithms, so long as they were not also memory intensive).

The main reason we utilized Java was to minimize debugging time and focus more on the development of the algorithms themselves. Unlike C ++, Java's static Math class provided most of the functionality we needed in order to calculate the complex request values of the function-based algorithms. Also, with the addition of template programing and for each loops in Java 5.0 and higher, it simplified the code for many strategies to a high degree. Lastly, Java's *Hashtable* and *PriorityQueue* classes supplied the most functionality.

Java's *PriorityQueue* class is an implementation of a binary heap. Many algorithms were able to take advantage of this data structure, decreasing the complexity for victim selection from $\Theta(n)$ to $\Theta(lg_2n)$. All function-based algorithms took advantage of this process. However, many function-based algorithms which rely on the time that has *passed* since the last reference to an object had to be recalculated at each invocation of the replacement strategy. Most of these algorithms' literature did not discuss appropriate means to calculate their request values efficiently in a timely manner. Bahn et al. [22] proved an efficient way in calculating the request value for LUV (Sect. 4.3.3.3), which used all the previous request times as opposed to a sliding window of request times like LNC-R-W3 (Sect. 4.3.3.3).

Algorithms which required a sliding window of K request times or relied on a certain history of the past reference times presented another challenge in our implementation as well. These algorithms were HLRU (Sect. 4.3.3.1), TSP (Sect. 4.3.3.4), and LNC-R-W3 (Sect. 4.3.3.4). At first thought, it would be easy to develop a linked list per object, but the extra space and time overhead in manipulating pointers demonstrated much inefficiency. A simple circular buffer cleared these inefficiencies and worked relatively fast. In fact, since the buffer needs only to be filled one way, it is only necessary to know where the next request must be placed, leading to one array of length K and a pointer to the oldest reference time in the buffer.

Two other algorithms, PSS (Sect. 4.3.3.1) and LRU-SP (Sect. 4.3.3.2), require a unique variable, ΔF_i, which measures the number of references that occurred since the last time an object i was referenced. Originally, a histogram was used and replayed back to see when and how many references occurred since the last time object i was referenced. There is sometimes a large time overhead in "replaying" this information through. A rather simple solution of giving each *request* a unique number, which followed that of the previous request, brought the complexity down to $\Theta(1)$. Then, in place for less space and time, we kept track of the last request number that referenced object i and the current request ID and were able to calculate ΔF_i with a simple subtraction.

The last detail to cover is the use of auxiliary caches, storing of past information about objects not currently cached. Though we ran a complete simulation set without auxiliary caches on most algorithms, we found algorithms like HLRU performed so poorly without the use of this information that they may have not existed at all. Thus, the auxiliary cache had to be implemented.

In our case, we did not delete information from the hash table, associated with the objects' URLs, when the object was evicted from the cache. This meant that all information about the objects was kept during the course of the simulation, which lead to large space complexities, and hence the memory intensive situations.

Normally, the auxiliary cache has its own cache strategies it applies, deleting information of unpopular objects over a certain time period. However, due to the short period our trace files contained (1 week), we decided that the time span was too small to apply any significant strategies to this information.

The algorithms which utilized the auxiliary cache information, and deemed memory intensive, are as follows: *HLRU, CSS, LRU-SP, GDSF, GD*, TSP, MIX, M-Metric, LNC-R-W3*, and *LUV*. No algorithms included in Section 4.4.3.2 made use of the auxiliary caches. Please refer to that section for a more thorough explanation.

4.4 Performance Metrics and Cost Models

4.4.1 Performance Metrics

Performance metrics are designed to measure different functional aspects of the Web cache. We used three measures. The first two have been used extensively before. The third one is a measure of how often the algorithm was invoked.

- **Hit rate**: This metric is used to measure all generic forms of caching. This is simply the number of *cache hits*, as defined in chap. 2, to the total number of *cacheable requests* seen by the proxy. It is important to realize that on average 35–55 % of the trace files we used were non-cacheable requests. Also important to note is the ratio of cache hits to total number of *requests* will produce the same ranking of strategies relative to this metric; however, the numbers are much smaller and, due to floating-point errors, are harder to separate and rank.
- **Byte-hit Rate:** This metric is similar to hit rate, except it emphasizes the total bytes saved by caching certain objects. Letting h_i be the total number of bytes saved from all *cache hits* that occur for an object i, r_i be the total number of bytes for all *cacheable requests* to object i, and n be the total number of unique objects seen in a request stream, then the byte-hit ratio is given by:

$$\frac{\sum_{i=0}^{n} h_i}{\sum_{i=0}^{n} r_i} \tag{4.18}$$

- **Object Removal Rate:** This metric came about as an observation of LRU-Min (Sect. 4.3.3.1) compared with other similar algorithms. Most algorithms operate under the assumption that disk access or CPU time is far less than the network latency needed to send the data to the client. However, on proxy servers such as those for university campuses or small businesses, the time to sort through 10,000 or more Web objects during the cache replacement strategy may be comparable with the network latency to the client. The object removal rate is essentially the measure of the amount of times the cache replacement strategy removes an object from a cache to the number of cacheable requests that occur. In a cache where watermarks may be set, this measure may tend to be very similar among many objects. However, in a cache where the replacement method is invoked when only necessary, this shows some surprising results of how well objects are at making the right decisions and how often they have to.

Letting k_i be the number of times object i was removed from the cache and z_i be the number of times object i was admitted to the cache, the object removal rate is given by:

$$\frac{\sum_{i=0}^{n} k_i}{\sum_{i=0}^{n} z_i} \qquad (4.19)$$

It is important to keep in mind that hit rate and the byte-hit ratio cannot be optimized for at the same time. No cache replacement strategy can be deemed as the best because there is a tendency in request streams for smaller documents to be requested more often than larger ones due to the download time it takes to gather these objects. Strategies that optimize for hit rate typically give preference to objects in a smaller size range, but in doing so tend to decrease byte-hit rate by giving less consideration to objects not in a particular size range.

A high removal rate may suggest several possibilities: that many small objects are being removed for larger objects, or that a poor decision is being made in relating object size to the number of objects to remove for that object. If the algorithm has a complex process per decision, then it is an indication that the algorithm may not be decreasing the number of documents or outside references the proxy has to make. However, it may be decreasing network latency as it may be giving preference to objects that have high latency/network costs, which is a factor the cost models use.

4.4.2 Cost Models

One of the most important characteristics of a Web object is the object's cost to fetch it from the origin server. There are several ways to relate a Web object to its cost. In this section, we will note all the different models we came across. Also, in the following, let S_i represents the size of a particular Web object i.

- **Uniform Model:** This assumes that the cost to fetch all objects is the same and so sets the costs of all objects to some constant greater than or equal to 1.
- **Byte Model:** This assumes that the network latency is the same for all servers, and so the only deciding factor in the cost for getting the object will be its size (as the size will decide the time to fetch the object). Thus, this method sets the cost to the size of the object.
- **Time Model:** This uses the past latency (download time) information to predict the future download time for an object. Thus, the object's cost is set to the predicted time it would take to fetch an object from a server. This has the unique advantage over the byte model in the rare occasion that small files that are on slow servers will have a higher cost, allowing them to have precedence over files that are similar in size. Since latency information cannot be gathered directly from the trace files, we

used the *Time Model* technique as shown by Hosseini-Khayat [23], which randomly assigns a time cost as:

$$C_i = x(q) + \frac{S_i}{y}, \tag{4.20}$$

where x is an exponential random variable representing network latency with a mean θ and y, which represents network throughput.

- **Network Cost**: This is similar to the byte model, but rather than predict future network latency and throughput, this simply estimates the number of packets that must be sent for a particular object. Thus, the cost based on the number of approximate packets for an object i is given by:

$$C_i = 2 + \left\lceil \frac{S_i}{536} \right\rceil \tag{4.21}$$

4.5 Experiment Setup and Results

4.5.1 Trace Files

In our experiment, we used trace files, which are files with recorded Web requests, to test each replacement strategy. The trace files were provided by IRCache [24]. These trace files are used in many previous proxy cache research, for example [2, 25–28], to mention a few. IRCache gathers their trace files and other data on Web caching from several different proxy servers located around the United States. More than enough information is provided in these files to indicate which requests were cacheable.

Originally, the trace files were provided with data spanning only a day of recorded Web requests. While some researchers in the literature used one hour or at the most day of request, we strung seven consecutive trace files together to create a week long trace file from each proxy that the data came from. Once this was done, we then "cleaned" the files to have only the cacheable requests (Refer to chap. 2 for a definition of a *cacheable request*) in them as to decrease the simulation time. We also exchanged each unique URL that appeared in the file with a unique integer identifier so that string comparison time could be decreased as well.

Table 4.3 presents statistics about the three traces we used for this simulation. These particular trace files were chosen due to their differences in size and cacheable request rates. Non-cacheable requests were extracted from the files prior to our experiment. Each trace represented varying levels of temporal locality, spatial locality, total bandwidth, and number of requests testing the various limits of the replacement strategies. All trace files represent one week of recorded requests caught by IRCache from 12:00 AM, Tuesday, July 10th, 2007 to 12:00 PM, Monday, July 16th, 2007. This reflects realistic Internet traffic.

Table 4.3 Trace file statistics for requests and bandwidth

Trace file	Urbana-champaign, Illinois (UC)	New York (NY)	Palo Alto, California (PA)
Total requests	2,485,174	1,457,381	431,844
Cacheable requests	55.31 %	51.70 %	23.61 %
Total bytes	71.99 GB	17.70 GB	5.601 GB
Cacheable bytes	95.62 %	90.55 %	88.30 %
Unique requests	1,306,758 (52.58 %)	708,901 (48.64 %)	241,342 (55.89 %)
Unique cacheable	73.78 % of unique requests	73.71 % of unique requests	33.89 % of unique requests

4.5.2 Simulation Setup and Parameters

The cost model we chose for our simulation was the time model, which produced similar results to both network and byte models. We used the same values as Hosseini [23] suggested, with the mean of the exponential variable, x, set to 1,000 ms and y being a uniform random variable between 1 byte/ms and 1,000 bytes/ms.

Some of the strategies presented in sect. 4.3 had one or more parameters. Table 4.4 shows a list of these strategies and their corresponding parameters. We ran several simulations of each strategy with different values for each parameter. In Sect. 5.3, we present only the instances of the parameters that reflected the best result for the corresponding strategy. If there is more than one parameter, Table 4.4 also shows the order these parameters are listed in the graphs of Sect. 6.3. For example, in Fig. 4.3, α-Aging (3,600,000/0.25) means that α-Aging performed best with interval = 3,600,000 ms (or 1 h) and $\alpha = 0.25$.

We simulated the algorithms with varying limits of the cache size available on the disk. We started at 50 MB (megabytes), then 100 MB, and finally ended with 200 MB. The reason for the small amount of disk space, when typical proxy cache servers might operate in terms of gigabytes, was to engage the cache replacement algorithm as frequently as possible. Also to note, as the maximum disk size allowed increased, all the replacement strategies performed better respective to each metric. However, the general increase in performance did not significantly change the ranking indexed by a particular metric in any of the simulations. For this reason, we will present the best instance of each strategy when the cache size was set to 200 MB. Significant differences for particular instances of strategies will be noted later.

Prior to running each test, we warmed up the cache with a smaller trace file from Boulder, Colorado. By using another trace file different from the others, we could guarantee that no files from that trace run would conflict with the other trace files. As a result, the cache would be filled by the time we started our simulation, putting our cache replacement strategies in effect immediately upon starting our tests. Therefore, all the results presented in Sect. 4.5.3 are the full results of the cache replacement strategies.

Table 4.4 Order and description of parameters in results

Strategy	Parameters
LRU-Threshold (Sect. 4.3.1)	Threshold: the maximum size threshold of the cache.
Pitkow/Reckers strategy (Sect. 4.3.1)	Interval: interval set to either daily or hourly describing when objects are differentiated by size.
HLRU (Sect. 4.3.1)	h: the hist value to use in a sliding window of h requests.
LFU-Aging (Sect. 4.3.2)	Average frequency threshold: the aging factor. Maximum frequency threshold: the maximum frequency counter of any given object.
α-Aging (Sect. 4.3.2)	Interval: interval, in ms, of when the aging factor is applied. α: the aging factor.
Segmented LRU (Sect. 4.3.3)	Protected Segment: the size, in percent of the total cache size of the protected segment.
Generational replacement (Sect. 4.3.3)	Generations: number of generations used.
Cubic selection scheme (Sect. 4.3.3)	Max Frequency: the maximum frequency counter, always a power of 2.
GD* (Sect. 4.3.4)	β: parameter describing reference correlation.
MIX (Sect. 4.3.4)	r_1, r_2, r_3, r_4: refer to Sect. 4.3.4 for more information.
M-Metric (Sect. 4.3.4)	f: frequency weight s: object size weight t: recency factor.
LNC-R-W3 (Sect. 4.3.4)	K: describes the size of the sliding window of past k requests. B: object size weight.
LUV (Sect. 4.3.4)	λ: describes an exponential scaling factor for $F(x)$

4.5.3 Simulation Results

First, we will present the results of individual strategies categorized as set by Sect. 4.2 for each metric. Then, as a global comparison, we will take the top three strategies from each category for a particular metric and compare them overall, to get a better sense of how the strategies from each category rank. After the presentation for each metric and trace file, we will discuss the results as a whole. Secondly, we will note peculiarities between different traces for individual strategies such as MIX (Sect. 4.3.3.4), M-Metric (Sect. 4.3.3.4), CSS (Sect. 4.3.3.3). Many strategies that utilized parameters will also need further analysis to see how different combinations of parameters affect the overall functionality. Lastly, we will discuss how certain attributes about the request streams affect certain strategies comparatively.

We have tested the reliability of these results by first validating our implementations of LRU and LFU. By running our simulation and verifying the results against a smaller version of a trace file and with smaller cache limits, we were able to compare the results against an expected result set.

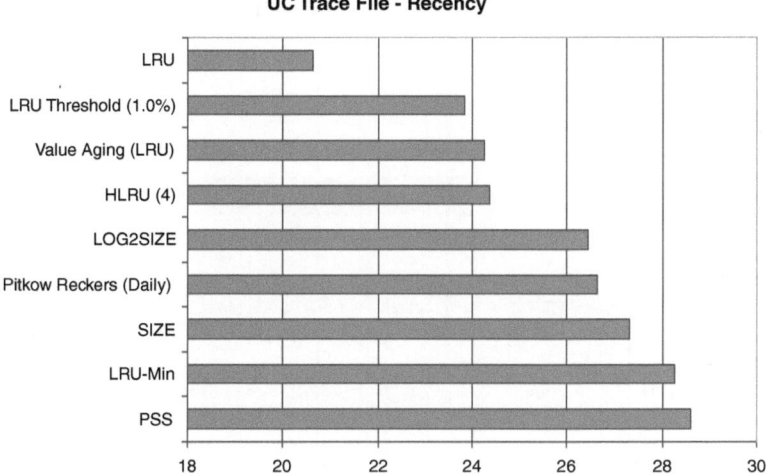

Fig. 4.2 Hit rate for recency using the UC trace file

The reader should note that the graphs presented in this research do not start at an origin of zero, and in fact, many of the graphs start at different origins. This was done to be able to graphically demonstrate our results in an easy to see and comparative manner. If the origin is at zero, most results would not be seen clearly. While some results are close, it is important to note that slight differences in percentage points of these metrics can equate to thousands of missed requests or bytes.

4.5.3.1 Hit Rate

Figures 4.2, 4.3, 4.4, and 4.5 show results for the recency, frequency, recency/ frequency, and function-based categories, respectively, using the UC trace file. Figures 4.6, 4.7, 4.8, and 4.9 show the results for the four categories using the PA trace, while Figs. 4.10, 4.11, 4.12, and 4.13 show those for NY trace files. Figures 4.14, 4.15, and 4.16 show the overall comparison of all strategies selecting the best three from each category, using The UC, PA, and NY trace files, respectively. Results of the recency category for the UC trace in Fig. 4.2 have a smaller variance compared with the PA trace in Fig. 4.6, demonstrating the effect of its high request rate.

In the recency category, PSS performed the best for UC, PA, and NY traces as shown in Figs. 4.2, 4.6, and 4.10, demonstrating that using recency along with grouping similar objects by size demonstrated its ability to intelligently remove the correct objects. However, the gain from its complicated decision process is questionable, as shown in the aforementioned figures, because simpler algorithms such as SIZE performed almost just as well. By examining Figs. 4.2, 4.6, and 4.10,

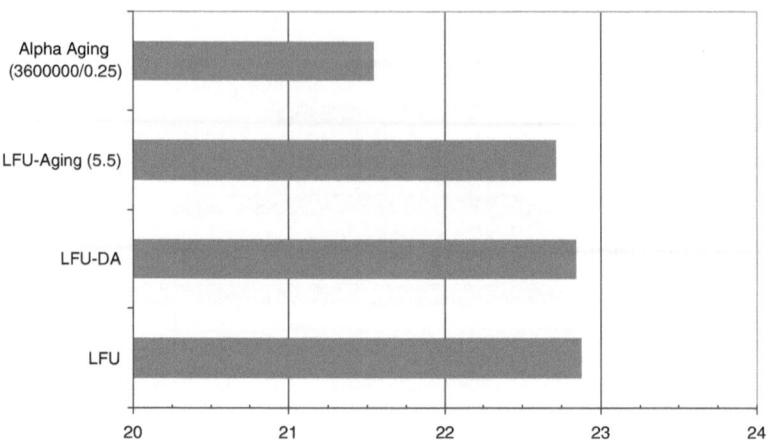

Fig. 4.3 Hit rate for frequency using the UC trace file

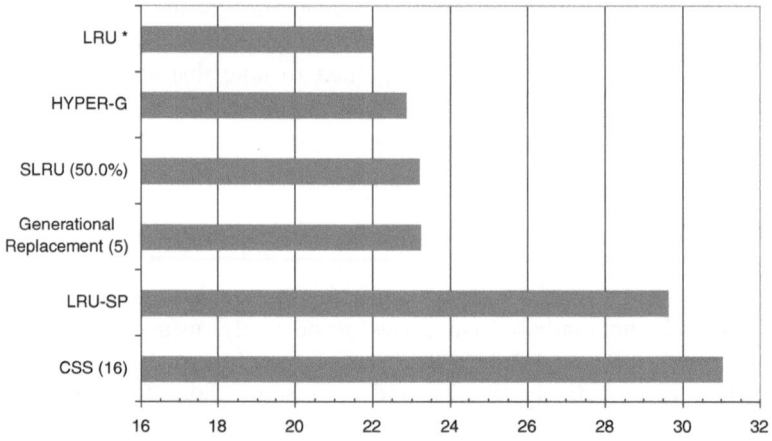

Fig. 4.4 Hit rate for frequency/recency using the UC trace file

one can clearly notice that among the recency category, the four algorithms, PSS, SIZE, LOG2-SIZE, and LRU-Min, did well consistently and demonstrate that when considering recency, size should also be considered at the same time for hit rate.

One can also notice from the 4 aforementioned figures that LRU, the parent strategy of the recency category, consistently did the worst. This is by far a revealing development because LRU is so widely used commercially in place of many of these other strategies. Simply considering the object size or using a little

UC Trace File - Function

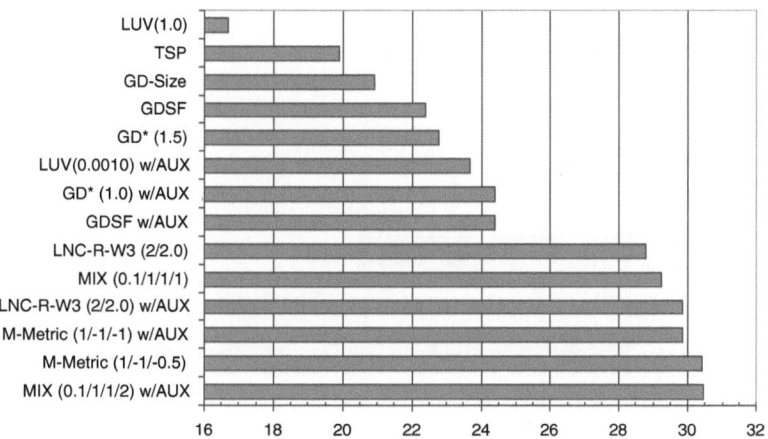

Fig. 4.5 Hit rate for frequency using the UC trace file

PA Trace File - Recency

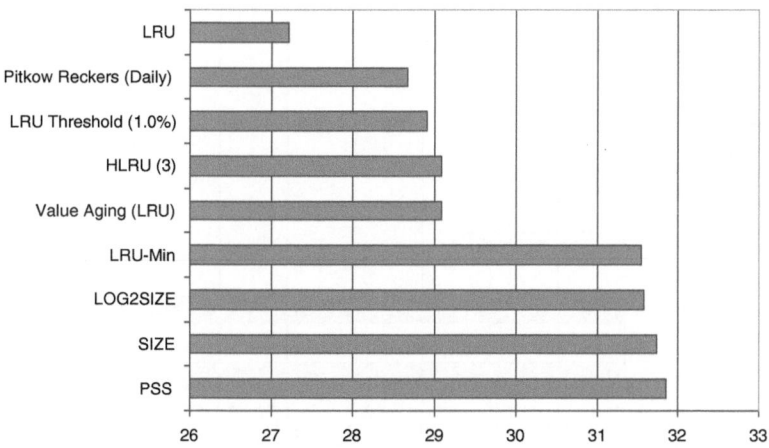

Fig. 4.6 Hit rate for recency using the PA trace file

more complicated strategy such as LRU-Min gains a considerable amount of performance over LRU; in conclusion, when recency is used as a base factor, derivative algorithms on other object characteristics will generally do far better.

This observation, however, does not apply to the frequency-based strategies. LFU as shown in Figs. 4.3, 4.7, and 4.11 always outperformed its derivative strategies. One reason may be that over the course of the simulated week, aging the frequency counters may not be needed since we used in-cache frequency. In that respect, when an object is removed, and if it should enter the cache again, it would

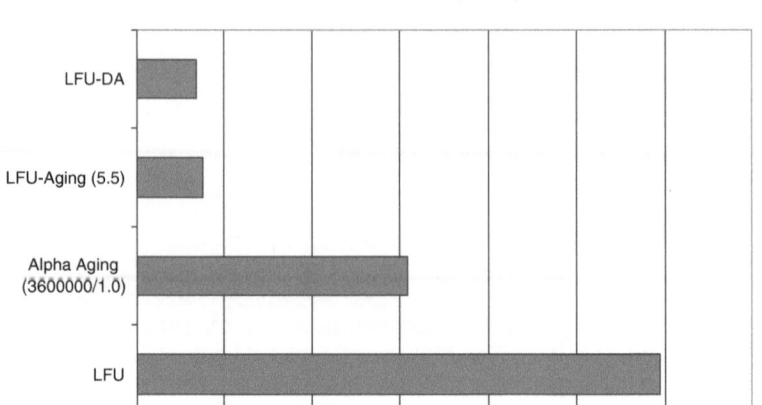

Fig. 4.7 Hit rate for frequency using the PA trace file

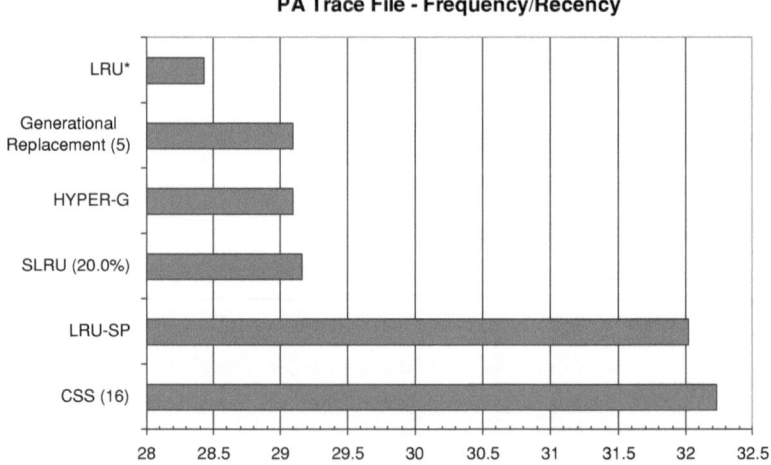

Fig. 4.8 Hit rate for frequency/recency using the PA trace file

have to accumulate its frequency count again; essentially, this is an aging factor in itself; though instead of being applied globally as LFU-DA and LFU-Aging attempt to do, it is applied when the object is removed; applying global aging factors on top of in-cache frequency may actually lead to an imbalanced weighting of frequency counts. Due to this flaw, the frequency strategies are always outperformed by the other categories' best in the overall charts as shown in Figs. 4.14, 4.15, 4.16.

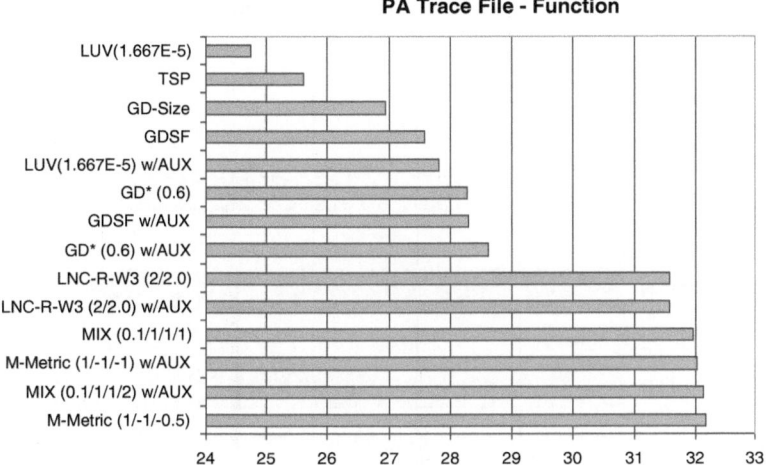

Fig. 4.9 Hit rate for function-based using the PA trace file

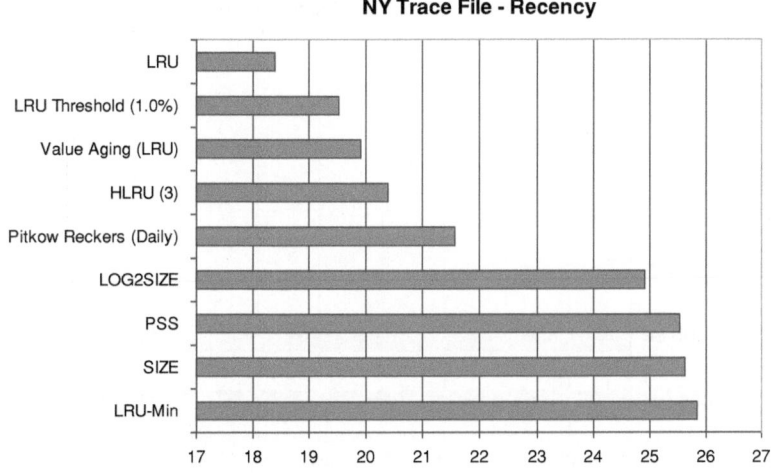

Fig. 4.10 Hit rate recency NY—200 MB

From Figs. 4.4, 4.8, and 4.12, it is clear that for frequency/recency strategies, however, that LRU-SP and CSS did the best consistently. Though it is not displayed here, CSS for any parameter generally did the same with an incredibly small variance (this is also true across all other metrics as well). LRU-SP generally did as well as PSS or a little better. With the exception of HYPER-G, all the algorithms did outperform LRU in hit rate, holding our earlier observation valid.

Figures 4.5, 4.9, and 4.13 show the results of hit rate for function-based strategies. These strategies hold the widest range of results. With the idea of

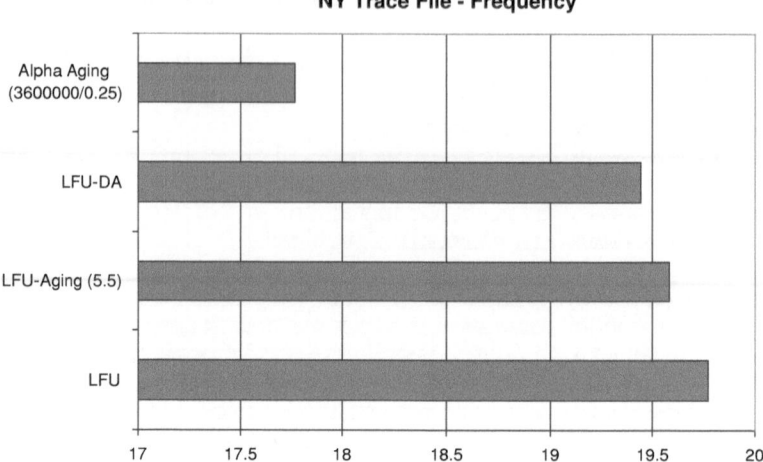

Fig. 4.11 Hit rate frequency NY—200 MB

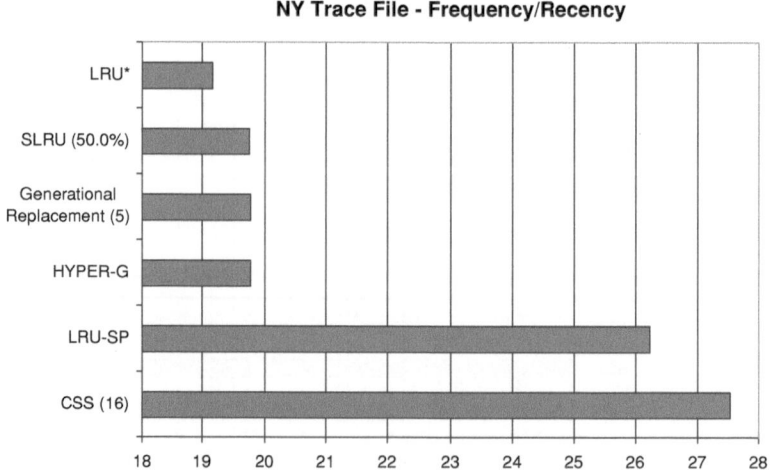

Fig. 4.12 Hit rate frequency/recency NY—200 MB

auxiliary caches, along with several different parameters, it should be of no surprise that these are the most complicated to implement and can require long durations of parameter tuning. An entire literature could explain the effect of each parameter on each of the appropriate algorithms, and yet, with the addition of a weighting factor such as that in GD* from GDSF, that it could be grounds for an entirely new strategy in of itself. In fact, MIX and M-Metric are so similar that in a uniform cost model, either could be used to model the other with the appropriate parameters.

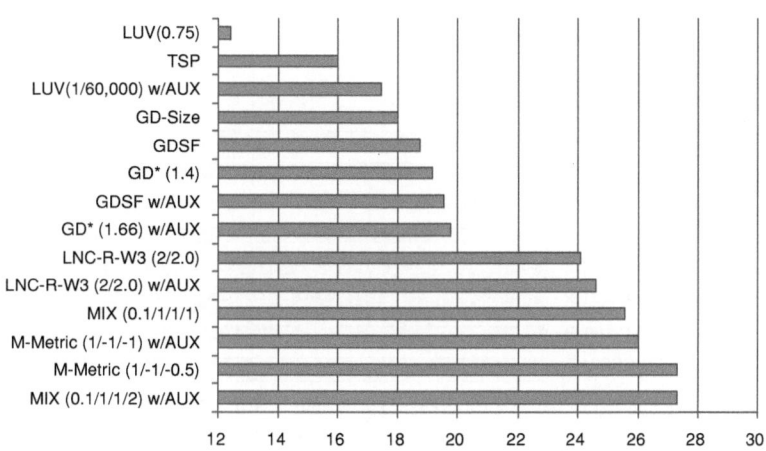

Fig. 4.13 Hit rate function NY—200 MB

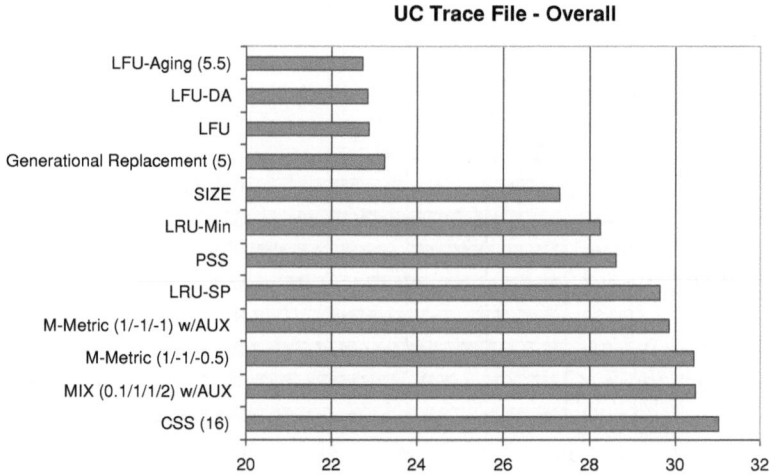

Fig. 4.14 Hit rate for overall using the UC trace file

Due to the nature of the parameters, what would perform well on one trace would almost certainly not be the same for the other traces. In an actual environment, this would require system administrators to be carefully tuning the metrics and be able to understand the parameter's relations to characteristics of the request stream. This would also require the use of some type of metric to measure characteristics of request streams, which though not discussed in this literature, that are as opposing as hit rate and byte-hit rate for most cases.

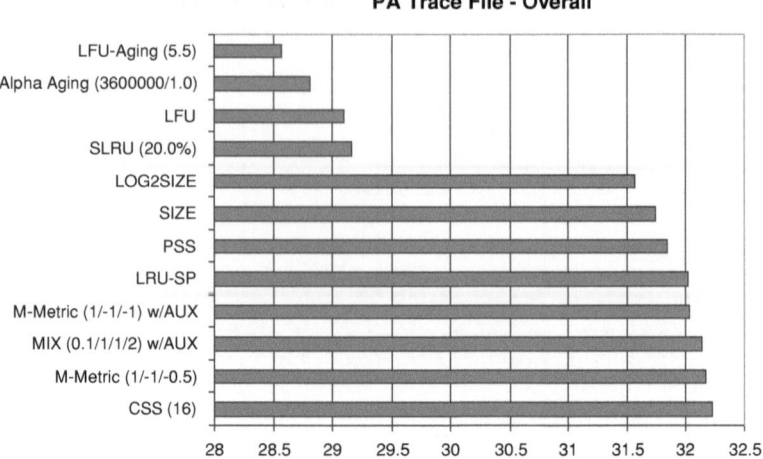

Fig. 4.15 Hit rate for overall using the PA trace file

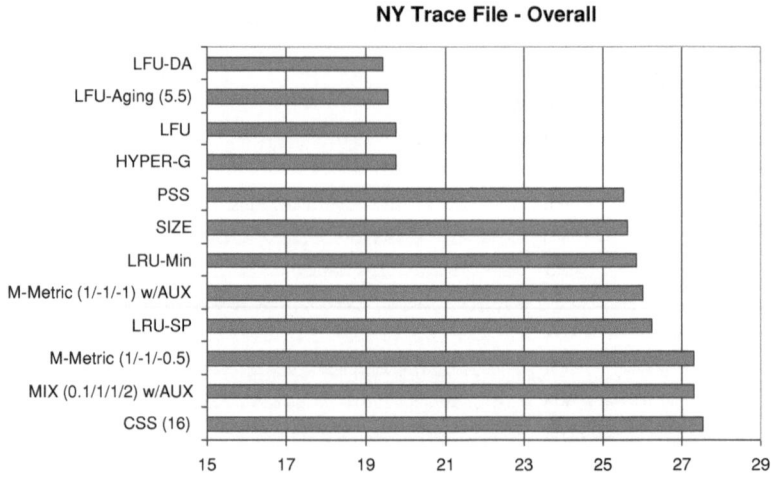

Fig. 4.16 Hit rate for overall using the NY trace file

Some general cases can be made for function-based strategies. The use of an auxiliary cache to keep further information on Web objects generally added to the hit rates of many strategies. The only exception to this was the M-Metric strategy. It is unclear as to why this oddity would occur in M-Metric and not in MIX with similar values, but the consideration of latency in MIX seems to have been enough where the addition of the auxiliary cache made all the difference.

We expected the results for cost-based algorithms to be lower than the rest for a rather simple reason when it came to hit rate: Users do not make judgments based on the latency cost of acquiring an object because in terms of those objects which are most frequently accessed (the smaller ones usually), the user may only feel a half a second lag. Relative to having to acquire a larger file, most users will ignore the delay for those objects which would affect hit rate the most. Thus, information pertaining to *latency* and/or *network* costs of acquiring an object will generally decrease the hit rate when used as a factor in the decision process.

Overall, Figs. 4.14, 4.15, and 4.16 show that CSS outperformed all other strategies consistently by utilizing a strong balance between size, frequency, and recency information to make its decisions. Followed closely by function-based strategies, which after parameter tuning will generally do almost as well at balancing characteristics, and as we will see later have the ability to capture more than just hit rate. When modified from LRU and SIZE, recency strategies clearly outperformed the frequency strategies (keep in mind that LFU outperformed LRU greatly). Frequency/recency strategies held their own, outperforming straight recency strategies on average.

4.5.3.2 Byte-Hit Rate

In previous literature, it has been noted that byte-hit rate tends to be inversely related to hit rate. If a strategy increases its hit rate, generally it will decrease its byte-hit rate. This is mainly due to the fact that larger Web objects are accessed less often because these files are updated less frequently and have high latency to acquire. Also, generally the network cost to access the object one time is much larger than most other files.

However, this is also an advantage to proxy caches because they can save large amounts of bandwidth with these assumptions as well. Objects with high cost and large size are generally targets for system administrators trying to cut down on bandwidth costs for servers. Thus, there is a trade-off between saving bandwidth and decreasing user perceived lag. In one, the users will feel the effects of the proxy cache, where as in the other, the origin servers will witness a cut in bandwidth costs.

Thus, it should be of no surprise that LOG2SIZE, SIZE, LRU-Min, and PSS, which did well under hit rate and perform the worst in byte-hit rate shown in Fig. 4.17. The one exception occurs in the PA trace file, Fig. 4.21. In fact, the exception occurs again in comparison with other categories in the PA trace results of Fig. 4.18 as well. LRU-SP derived from PSS also has similar effects. These out of line occurrences may be due to the fact that the PA trace file has a sparse request stream with less than a quarter of cacheable requests. Strategies that relatively compare objects' characteristics adapt to density of request streams as opposed to completely falling out. Also, strategies that compare static characteristics, characteristics that do not vary much over the course of the simulation, also tend to do well on sparse request streams. For instance, M-Metric and MIX represented in Fig. 4.20 are outperformed by the Greedy-Dual derivatives and LNC-R-W3. However, it should be noted that the majority of function-based strategies greatly

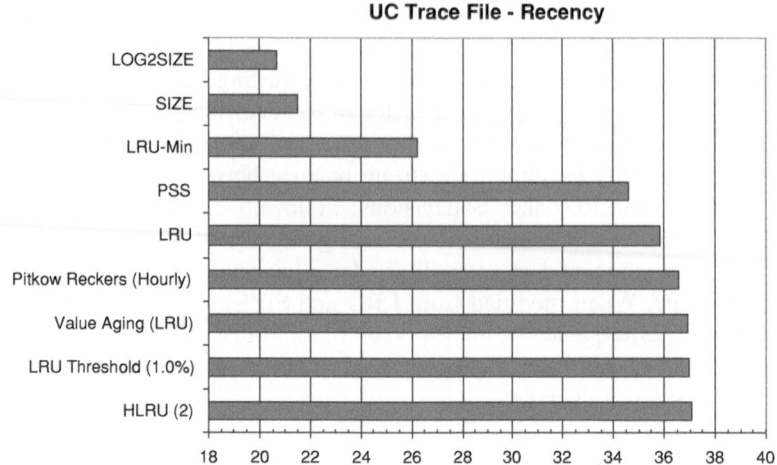

Fig. 4.17 Byte-hit rate for recency using the UC trace file

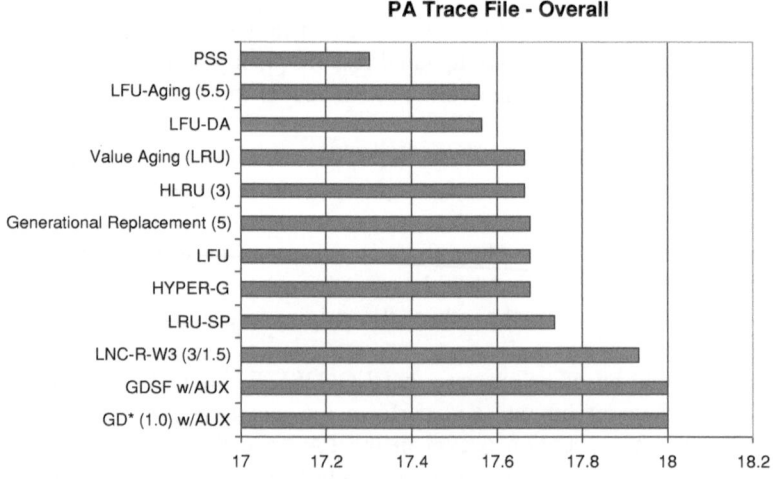

Fig. 4.18 Byte-hit rate for overall using the PA trace file

outperform many of the other categories and as well have a low deviation from one another Fig. 4.19.

Another observation is that HLRU does well in the UC trace, Fig. 4.17, and NY trace, Fig. 4.21, and also manages to do the best for the PA's Recency set, Fig. 4.22. This may suggest that considering when the past hth request (Sect. 4.3.1) occurred is somehow relevant to the size of objects. Value-Aging also did fairly

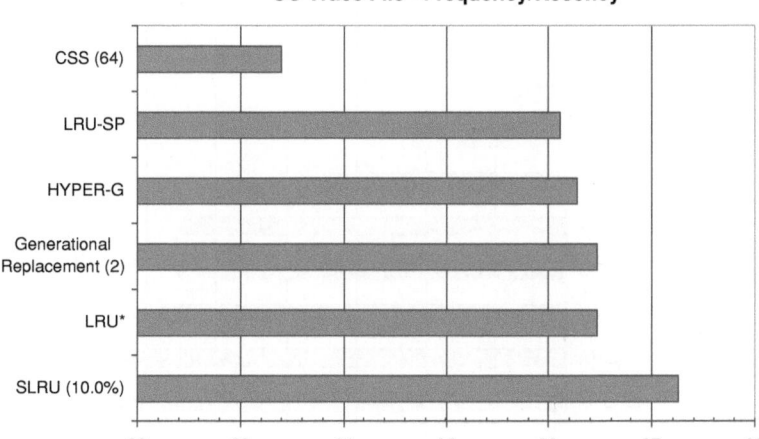

Fig. 4.19 Byte-hit rate for frequency/recency using the UC trace file

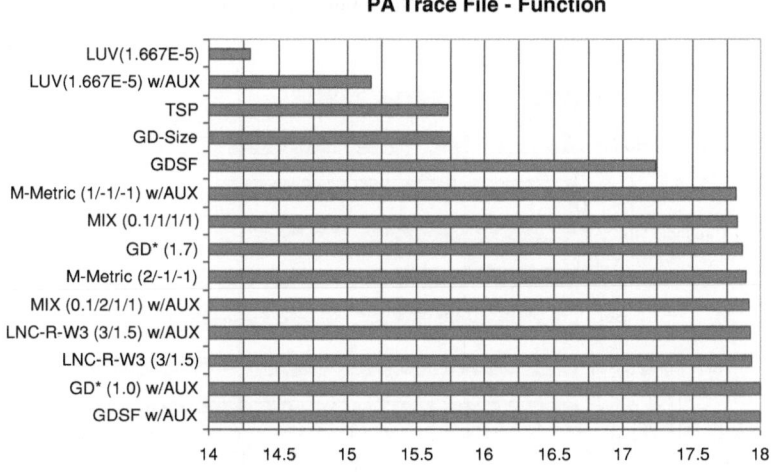

Fig. 4.20 Byte-hit rate function PA

well in comparison with other recency strategies, but did only mediocre overall. This is most likely due to the fact that Value-Aging slowly increases as the time grows, which is an advantage to larger objects, which tend to have long periods between requests Fig. 4.23.

In terms of function-based strategies, Figs. 4.24, 4.20, and 4.25 all represent a different ranking between one another. For UC, Fig. 4.24, MIX on top, PA, Fig. 4.20, with GD* and GDSF and NY, Fig. 4.25, with LNC-R-W3 and GD*. However, all had LNC-R-W3 in the top three. This makes sense since HLRU did

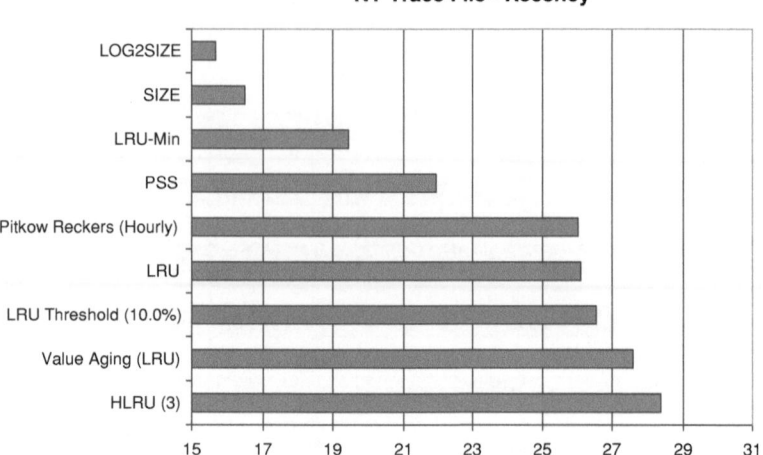

Fig. 4.21 Byte-hit rate recency NY—200 MB

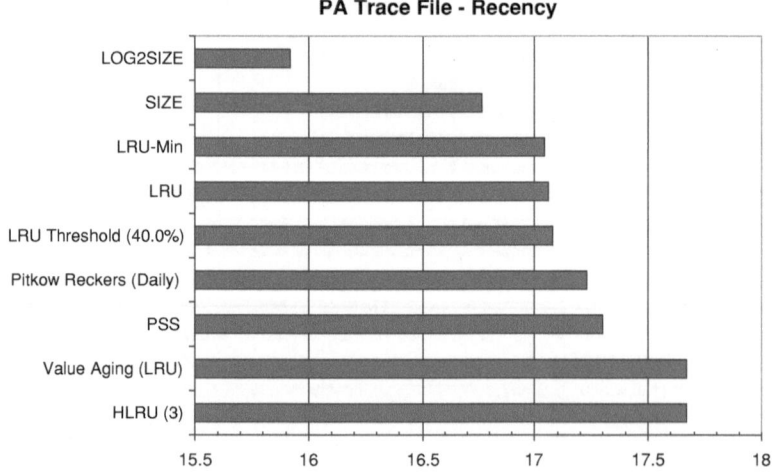

Fig. 4.22 Byte-hit rate for recency using the PA trace file

well in recency, which utilizes a sliding window scheme of h requests like LNC-R-W3. However, LNC-R-W3 also uses information about frequency and size, which enhances its comparisons over HLRU to optimize primarily for byte-hit rate Fig. 4.23

In terms of the frequency class, Figs. 4.26, 4.28, and 4.29, LFU-Aging seems to perform well. Again, the frequency-based methods did worse overall, Figs. 4.30 and 4.31, but it is still too little data to rule out frequency as being an irrelevant characteristic, as LFU still outperforms LRU each simulation. Also, the aging

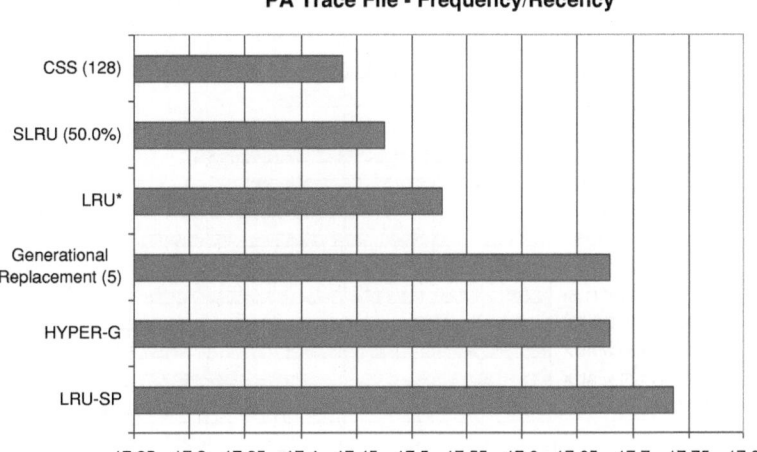

Fig. 4.23 Byte-hit rate for frequency/recency using the PA trace File

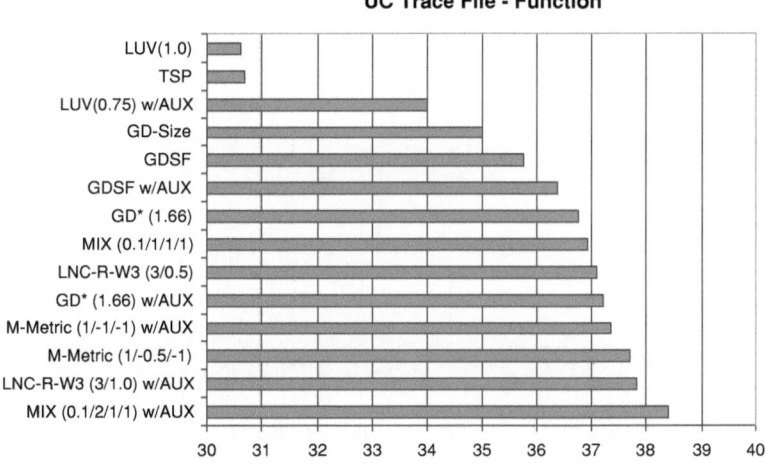

Fig. 4.24 Byte-hit rate using the UC trace file

factors for LFU-DA and LFU-Aging, which were a problem for hit rates, actually work to the advantage of large objects under byte-hit rate. In this condition, since no frequency counter can be less than 1, usually the aging factors have no effect on large objects when the aging factors have been applied; thus, the objects with higher frequencies are brought down in comparison with the large objects giving some larger objects an equal chance to stay in the cache as their smaller counterparts Fig. 4.27.

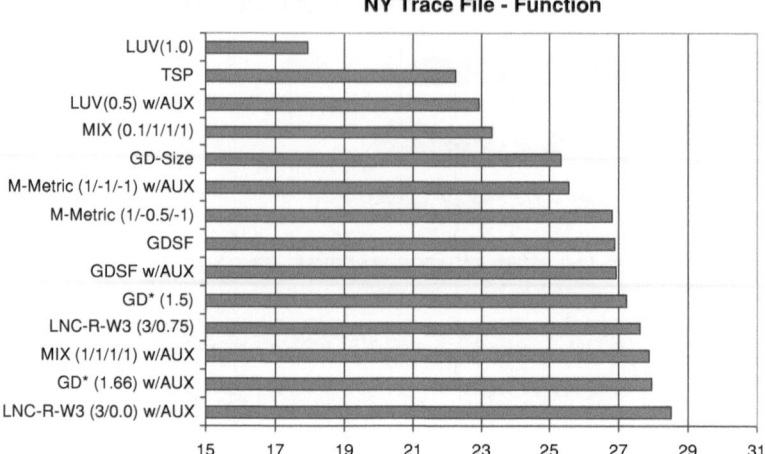

Fig. 4.25 Byte-hit rate function NY

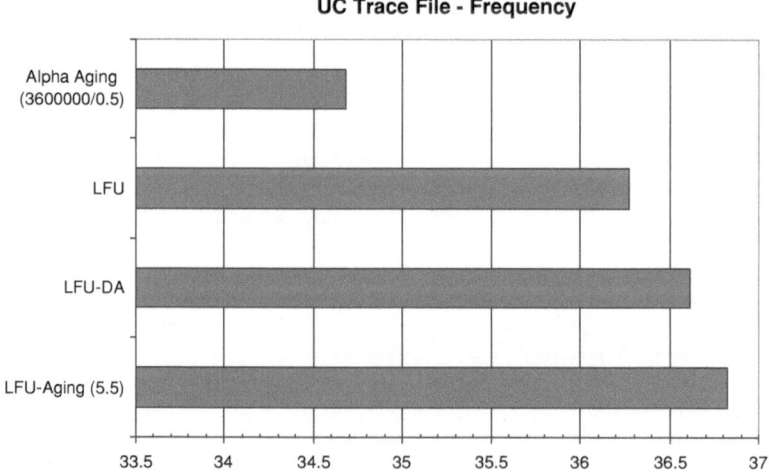

Fig. 4.26 Byte-hit rate for frequency using the UC trace file

4.5.3.3 Removal Rate

The removal rate highlights a third trade-off with respect to the proxy server itself. As stated in Sect. 5.1, removal rates can be a significant indicator of CPU usage and storage accesses. For a high removal rate, generally we can assume that the strategy on average exchanges smaller objects for larger objects. A low removal rate suggests that the strategy removes larger objects first in exchange for the placement of many smaller objects.

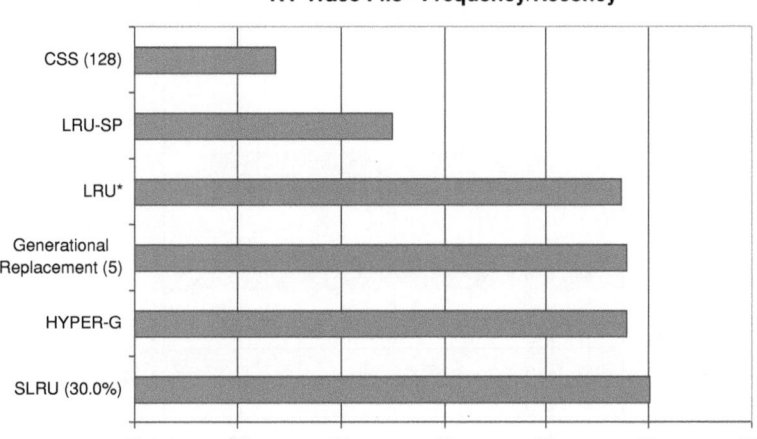

Fig. 4.27 Byte-hit rate frequency/recency NY

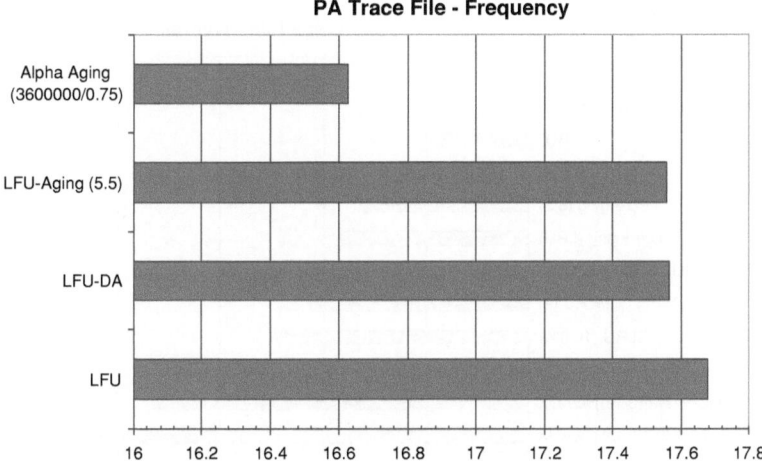

Fig. 4.28 Byte-hit rate for frequency using the PA trace file

Clearly, under these assumptions, SIZE and other similar strategies that performed well under hit rate but not so well in byte-hit rate will perform optimally here. This suggests that hardware will be in more use to serve the users more than save on bandwidth, which has a greater effect on the origin servers. In this strategy, smaller objects are constantly swapped for other equally sized objects, while larger objects are removed first before smaller ones Fig. 4.32

Figures 4.33, 4.34, 4.35, 4.36, 4.37, 4.38, 4.39, 4.40, 4.41, 4.42, 4.43, 4.44, 4.45, and 4.46 show the removal rates for our simulations. Figures 4.33, 4.34, 4.35,

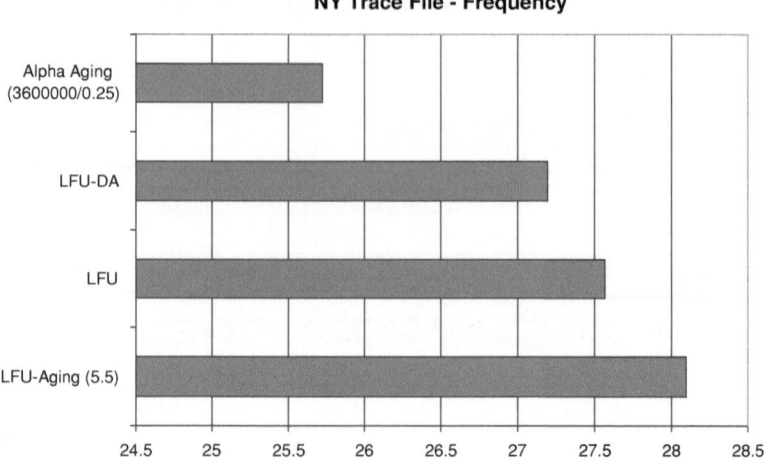

Fig. 4.29 Byte-hit rate frequency NY—200 MB

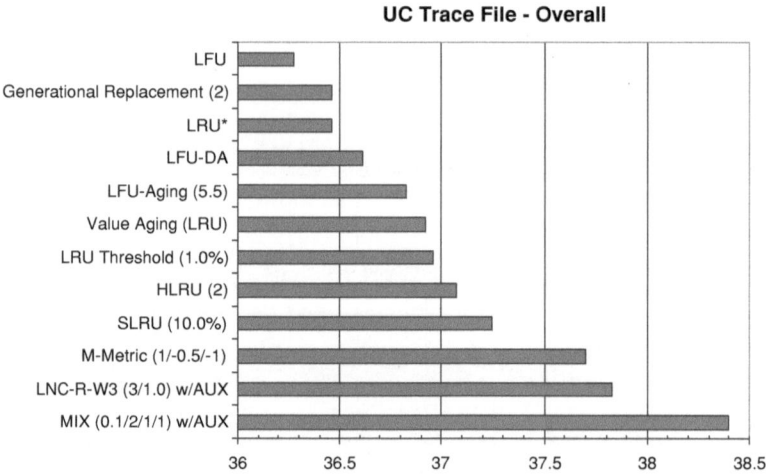

Fig. 4.30 Byte-hit rate for overall using the UC trace file

and 4.36 show the results for the recency, frequency, recency/frequency, and function-based categories, respectively, using the UC trace file. Figures 4.37, 4.38, 4.39, and 4.40 show the results for the four categories using the PA trace, while Figs. 4.41, 4.42, 4.43, and 4.44 show those for NY trace files. Figure 4.45 shows the overall comparison of all strategies selecting the best three from each category, using the UC, PA, and NY trace files, respectively.

In the function-based strategies, Figs. 4.35, 4.39, and 4.43, the strategies follow the general rankings as set by the byte-hit rate. However, an odd occurrence in

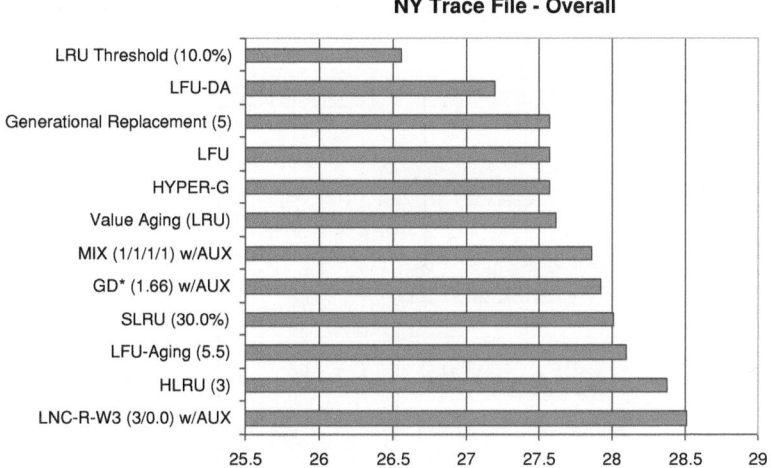

Fig. 4.31 Byte-hit rate for overall using the NY trace file

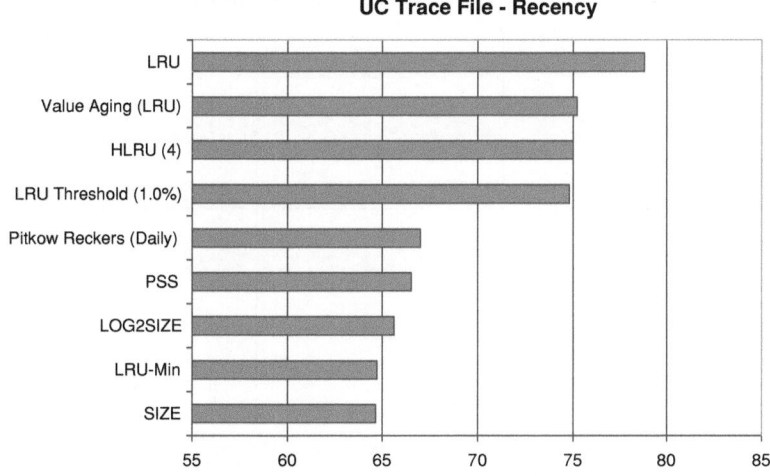

Fig. 4.32 Removal rate recency UC

PA's trace file, Fig. 4.39, shows that the deviation between the highest and lowest simulations is between 50 and 60 %. It is an interesting occurrence because in hit rate, Fig. 4.9, the most deviation is about 5–7 % of the highest and lowest, and the byte-hit rate, Fig. 4.24, has an even smaller deviation. NY trace results have a much larger deviation on both and yet a rather stable removal rate.

This suggests that while deviations of hit rates and byte-hit rates may be low, there is no clear pattern between removal rate and the other two metrics *despite*

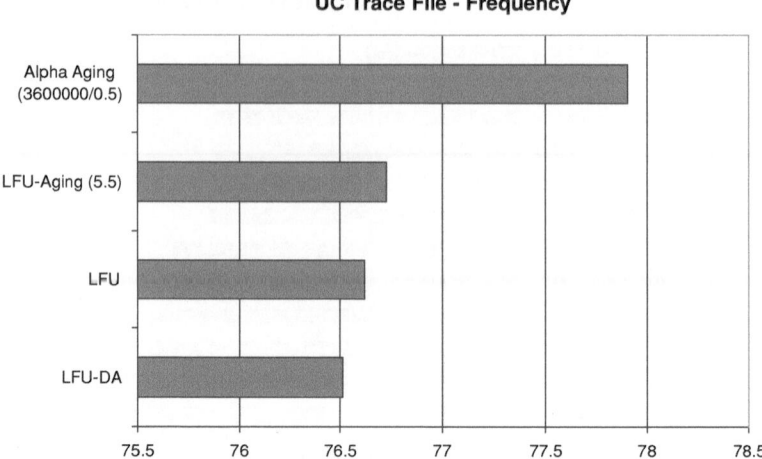

Fig. 4.33 Removal rate frequency UC

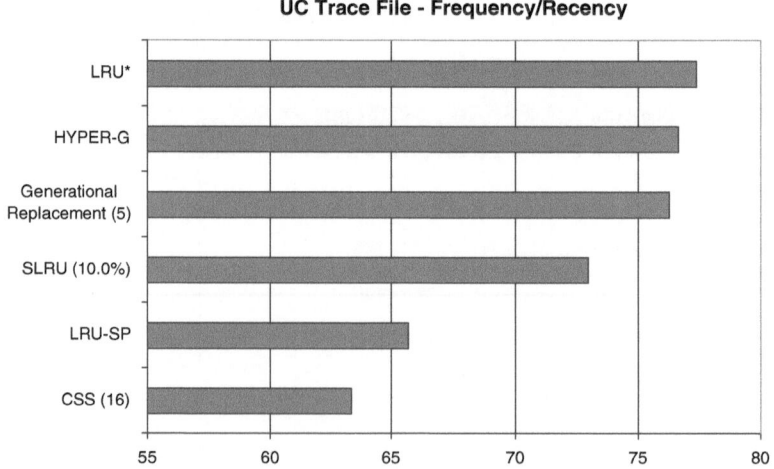

Fig. 4.34 Removal rate frequency/recency UC

that it generally may otherwise. In the case of PA's results, it would be a much wiser decision based on a sparse request stream, to implement M-Metric and MIX because they will have less drive access, making smarter decisions about which objects to replace while having almost identical byte-hit rate to Greedy-Dual's derivations and doing far better in hit rate than other function-based methods.

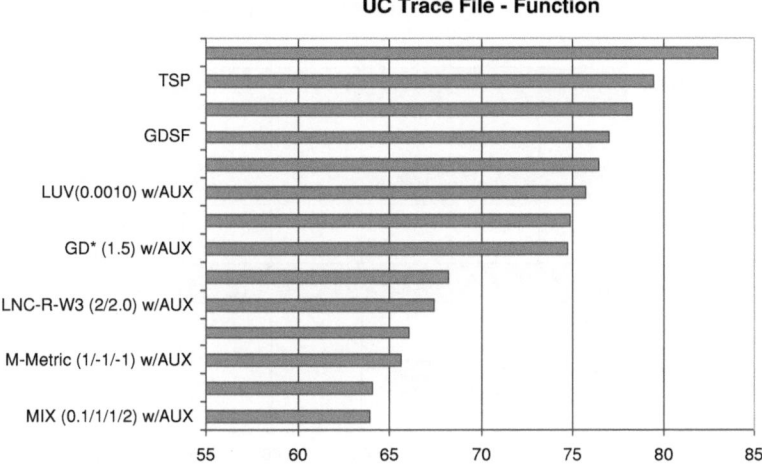

Fig. 4.35 Removal rate function UC

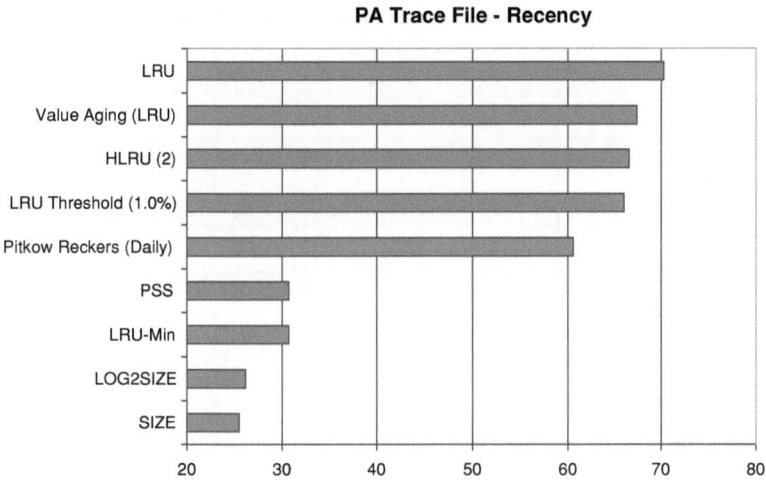

Fig. 4.36 Removal rate recency PA

4.6 Conclusion

Proxy servers have been used extensively to reduce network traffic and improve availability and scalability of the network. We have shown how one aspect of the Web cache, the cache replacement strategy, can adversely affect the performance. This research has provided an exhaustive quantitative analysis of cache replacement strategies based on three metrics. The metrics are very important as they

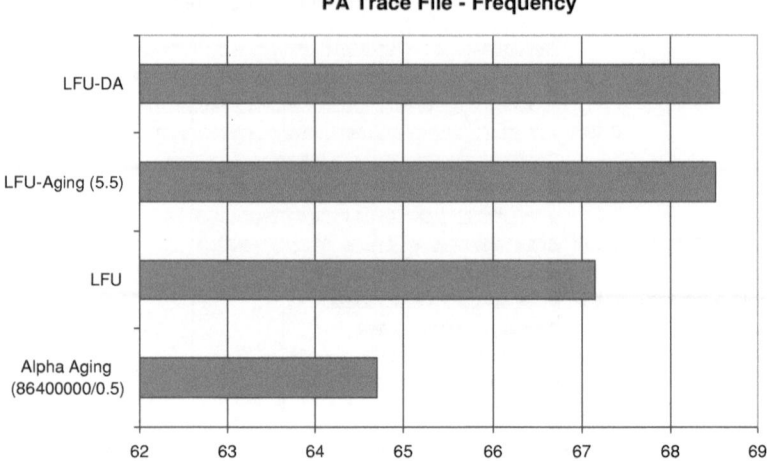

Fig. 4.37 Removal rate frequency PA

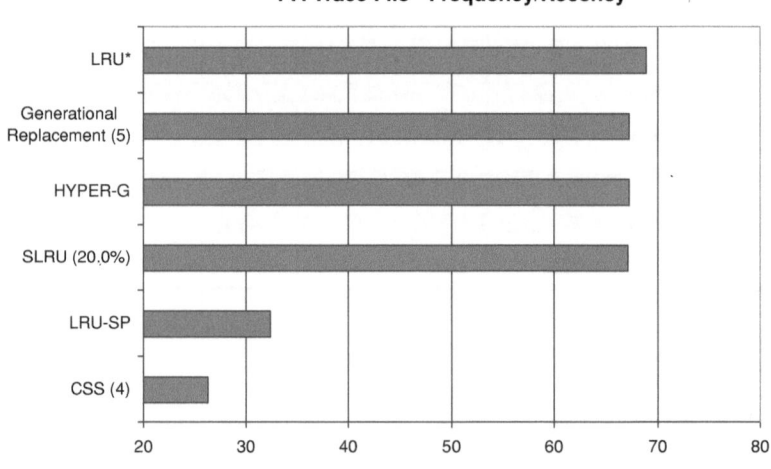

Fig. 4.38 Removal rate frequency/recency PA

indicate the amount of bandwidth (or network traffic), user perceived lag (or delay time), and CPU usage (or disk access).

A comprehensive study of twenty-seven algorithms was included along with details of their implementation. First, we presented the results of individual strategies categorized as recency, frequency, recency/frequency, and function based for three different trace files and three different metrics. Then, as a global comparison, we took the top three strategies from each category for a particular

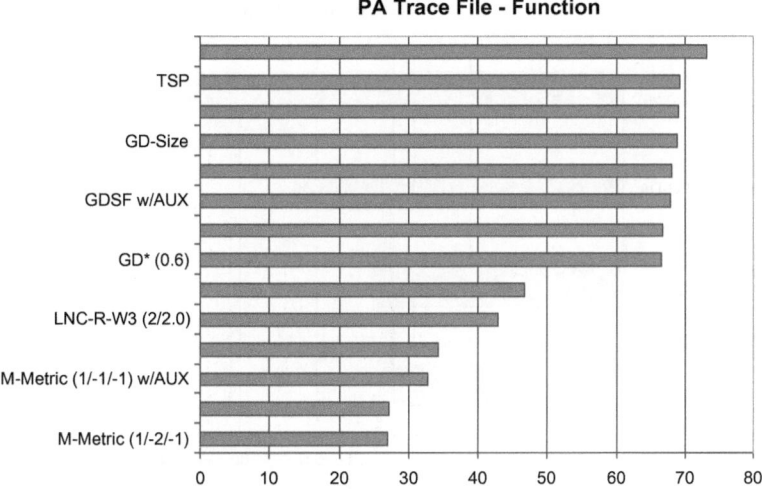

Fig. 4.39 Removal rate function PA

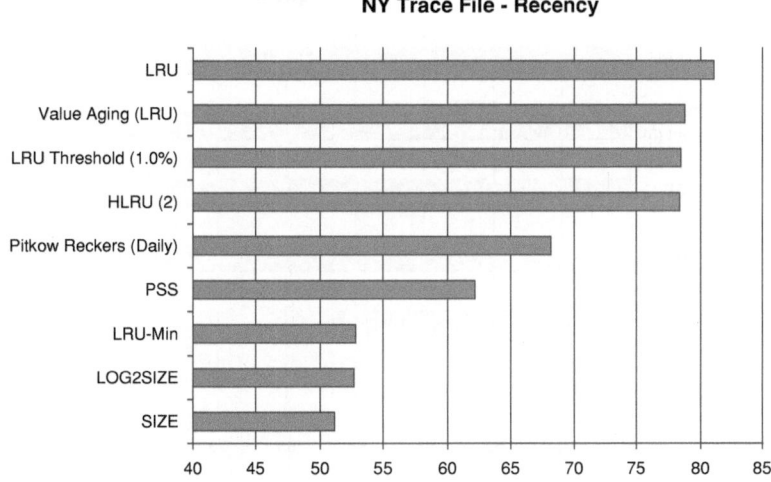

Fig. 4.40 Removal rate recency NY

metric and compared them overall, to get a better sense of how the strategies from each category rank. Secondly, we noted peculiarities between different traces for individual strategies. Many strategies that utilized parameters needed further analysis to see how different combinations of parameters affect the overall functionality. We discussed how certain attributes about the request streams affect certain strategies comparatively. Several explanations were provided detailing

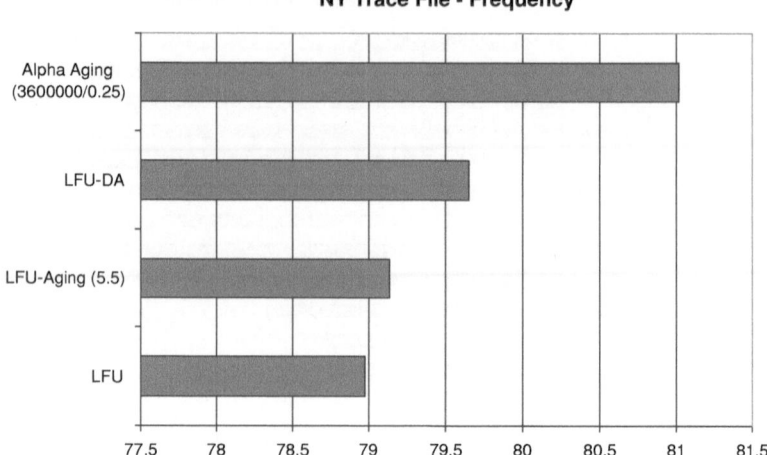

Fig. 4.41 Removal rate frequency NY

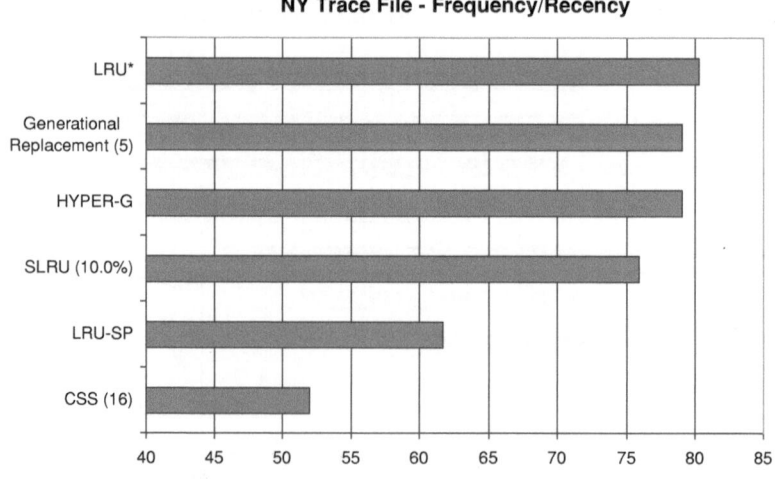

Fig. 4.42 Removal rate frequency/recency NY

various performance issues of the strategies individually and as a category. We also demonstrated that the sparseness of request streams has a large effect on an algorithm's performance and that some algorithms thought to be resilient to temporal locality, such as many function-based methods, were far more sensitive than previously thought.

The Squid proxy server provides a choice between LFU-DA, GDSF, a heap-based variation of LRU, and by default enables a linked list version of its LRU

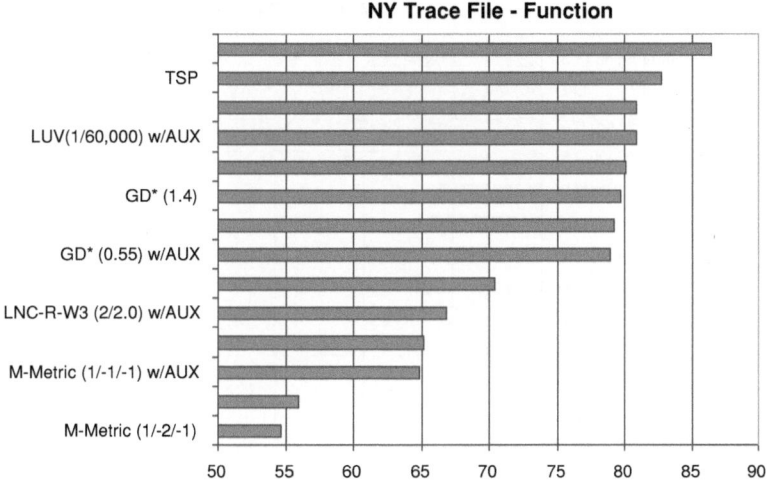

Fig. 4.43 Removal rate function NY

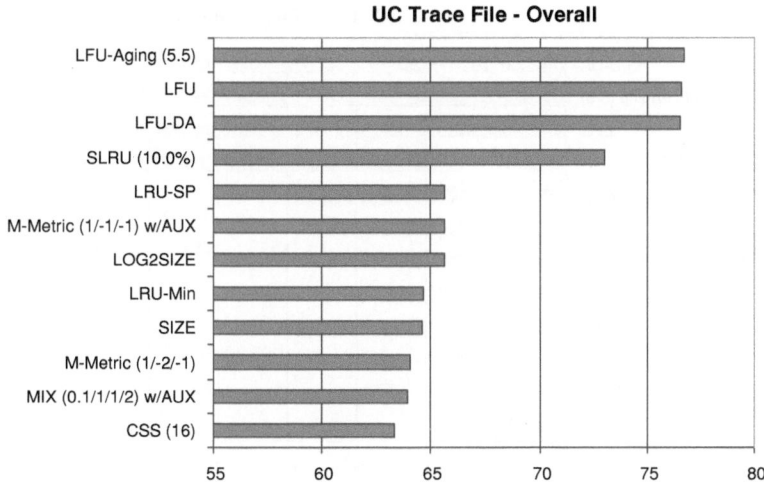

Fig. 4.44 Removal rate overall UC

variant. Based on the research presented in this research, it is obvious that algorithms like PSS, CSS, M-Metric, MIX, and GDSF would allow system administrators greater control over their proxy servers. System administrators should configure Squid to use one of the more advanced strategies, GDSF or LFU-DA, instead of the default LRU that was clearly demonstrated to perform the worst consistently in our research.

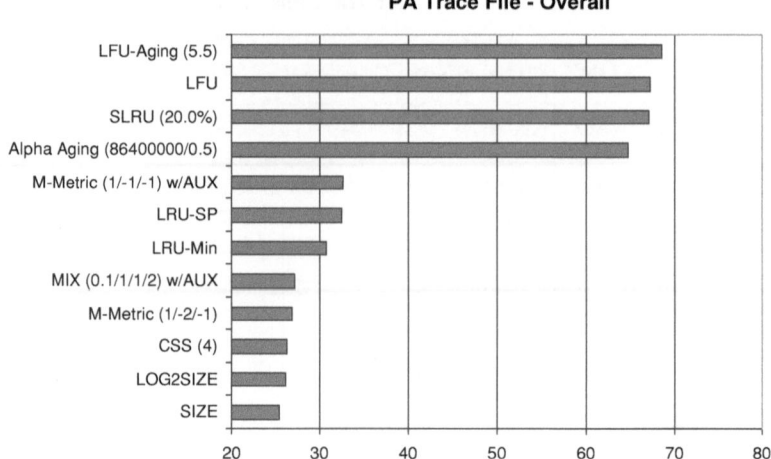

Fig. 4.45 Removal rate overall PA

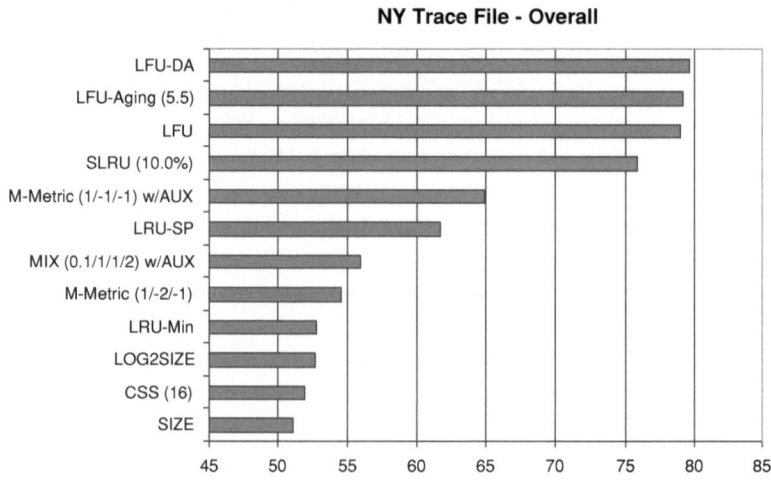

Fig. 4.46 Removal rate overall NY

Most of the strategies we covered are relatively simple to implement and incorporate a relative low CPU and space overhead and should be deployed in commercial proxy cache servers to allow system administrators and ISPs greater control over the QoS of their services. Our results are particularly important in ad hoc wireless networks where mobile devices have limited cache size.

References

1. S. Podlipnig, L. Boszormenyi, A survey of web cache replacement strategies. ACM Comput. Surv. **35**(4), 374–398 (2003)
2. K. Wong, Web cache replacement policies: A pragmatic approach. IEEE Network **20**(1), 28–34 (2006)
3. M. Abrams, C.R. Standridge, G. Abdulla S. Williams, E. Fox, Caching proxies: Limitations and potentials, in *Proceedings of the 4th International World Wide Web Conference*, 1995
4. J. Pitkow, M. Recker, A simple yet robust caching algorithm based on dynamic access patterns, in *Proceedings of the 2nd International World Wide Web Conference*, pp. 1039–1046, 1994
5. S. Williams, M. Abrams, C.R. Standridge, G. Abdulla, E.A. Fox, Removal policies in network caches for world-wide web documents, in *Proceedings of ACM SIGCOMM*. ACM Press, New York, pp. 293–305, 1996
6. J. Zhang, R. Izmailov, D. Reinniger, M. Ott, Web caching framework: Analytical models and beyond, in *Proceedings of the IEEE Workshop on Internet Applications*. IEEE Computer Society, Piscataway, NJ, 1999
7. A. Vakali, Proxy cache replacement algorithms: A history-based approach. World Wide Web **4**(4), 277–297 (2001)
8. C.C. Aggarwal, J.L. Wolf, P.S. Yu, Caching on the World Wide Web, IEEE Trans. Know. Data Eng., **11**, 94–107 (1999)
9. M.F. Arlitt, L. Cherkasova, J. Dilley, R.J. Friedrich, T.Y. Jin, Evaluating content management techniques for web proxy caches, ACM SIGMETRICS Perform. Evaluation. **27**, 3–11, (2000)
10. M.F. Arlitt, R.J. Friedrich, T.Y. Jin, Performance Evaluation of web proxy cache replacement policies, Tech. rep. HPL-98-97(R.1), Hewlett-Packard Company, Palo Alto, CA (1999)
11. N. Osawa, T. Yuba, K. Hakozaki, Generational Replacement schemes for a WWW proxy server, High-Performance Computing and Networking (HPCN'97). Lecture Notes in Computer Science, vol 1225 (Springer, Berlin, 1997) pp. 940–949
12. C.-Y. Chang, T. McGregor, G. Holmes, The LRU* WWW proxy cache document replacement algorithm, in *Proceedings of the Asia Pacific Web Conference*, 1999
13. I. Tatarinov, An efficient LFU-like policy for web caches, Tech. Rep. NDSU-CSORTR-98-01, Computer Science Department, North Dakota State University, Wahpeton, ND (1998)
14. K. Cheng, Y. Kambayashi, A size-adjusted and popularity-aware LRU replacement algorithm for web caching, in *Proceedings of the 24th International Computer Software and Applications Conference (COMPSAC)*. IEEE Computer Society, Piscataway, NJ, pp. 48–53, 2000
15. P. Cao, S. Irani, Cost-aware WWW proxy caching algorithms, in *Proceedings of the USENIX Symposium on Internet Technologies and Systems*. pp. 193–206, 1997
16. S. Jin, A. Bestavros, GreedyDual*: Web caching algorithms exploiting the two sources of temporal locality in web request streams, in *Proceedings of the 5th International Web Caching and Content Delivery Workshop*. 2000
17. M.F. Arlitt, L. Cherkasova, J. Dilley, R.J. Friedrich, T.Y. Jin, Evaluating content management techniques for web proxy caches, ACM SIGMETRICS Perform Evaluation Rev. **27**, 3–11 (2000)
18. Q. Yang, H.H. Zhang, H. Zhang, Taylor series prediction: a cache replacement policy based on second-order trend analysis, in *Proceedings of the 34th Hawaii International Conference on Systems Sciences*. IEEE Computer Society, Piscataway, NJ. 2001
19. N. Niclausse, Z. Liu, P. Nain, A new efficient caching policy for the world wide web, in *Proceedings of the Workshop on Internet Server Performance*, pp. 119–128 (1998)
20. D. Wessels, Intelligent caching for World-Wide-Web objects, M.S. thesis, University of Colorado at Boulder, Boulder, CO (1995)

21. P. Scheuermann, J. Shim, R. Vingralek, A case for delay-conscious caching of web documents, in *Proceedings of the 6th International WWW Conference* (1997)
22. H. Bahn, K. Koh, S.L. Min, S.H. Noh, Efficient replacement of nonuniform objects in web caches. IEEE Comput. **35**, 65–73 (2002)
23. S. Hosseini-Khayat, Investigation of generalized caching, Ph.D. dissertation. Washington University, St. Louis, MO (1997)
24. IRCache Home,http://www.ircache.net/ Accessed 11 Nov 2007
25. A. Abhari, A. Serbinski, M. Gusic, Improving the performance of apache web server, in Proceedings of the 2007 spring simulation multiconference, Vol 1, pp. 166–169 (2007)
26. G.P. Sajeev, M.P. Sebastian, A novel content classification scheme for web caches, Evolving Systems, (2010). doi: 10.1007/s12530-010-9026-6
27. R.P. Doyle, J.S. Chase, S. Gadde, A.M. Vahdat, The trickle-down effect: web caching and server request distribution, Comput. Commun., **25**(4), 345–356 (2002)
28. S. Gadde, J. Chase, M. Rabinovich, Web caching and content distribution: A view from the interior, in Proceedings of the 5th international web caching and content delivery workshop, Lisbon, Portugal (May 2000)
29. B. Davison, A web caching primer. IEEE Internet Comput. **5**(4), 38–45 (2001)
30. M. Arlitt, A performance study of internet web servers, M.SC. Thesis, University of Saskatchewan (1996)

Chapter 5
Web Proxy Cache Replacement Scheme Based on Backpropagation Neural Network

Keywords Neural network proxy cache replacement (NNPCR) · Web proxies · Proxy caching · Neural networks · Replacement algorithm · Performance evaluation · Training and simulation · Hit rate · Byte-hit rate · Trace file · IRCache

5.1 Introduction

This chapter presents how neural networks are trained to classify cacheable objects from real-world data sets using information known to be important in web proxy caching, such as frequency and recency. Correct classification ratios (CCRs) between 0.85 and 0.88 are obtained both for data used for training and for data not used for training. Our approach is compared with least recently used (LRU), least frequently used (LFU) and the optimal case which always rates an object with the number of future requests. Performance is evaluated in simulation for various neural network structures and cache conditions. The final neural networks achieve hit rates that are 86.60 % of the optimal in the worst case and 100 % of the optimal in the best case. Byte-hit rates are 93.36 % of the optimal in the worst case and 99.92 % of the optimal in the best case. We examine the input-to-output mappings of individual neural networks and analyze the resulting caching strategy with respect to specific cache conditions.

The rest of the chapter is organized as follows. Section 5.2 discusses a novel proxy cache replacement scheme that incorporates neural networks. Section 5.3 explains the methods and metrics used for simulation and results analysis. Section 5.3 presents the results of this research, while Sect. 5.4 provides the summary and conclusions.

H. ElAarag, *Web Proxy Cache Replacement Strategies*,
SpringerBriefs in Computer Science, DOI: 10.1007/978-1-4471-4893-7_5,
© Hala ElAarag 2013

5.2 Neural Network Proxy Cache Replacement

In this section, we present our neural network proxy cache replacement (NNPCR) technique. The main idea behind NNPCR is to construct and train a multi-layer feed-forward artificial neural network to handle web proxy cache replacement decisions. The likelihood of a future request for a web object is taken as an unknown function. A neural network is constructed to approximate this unknown function. The network is trained to approximate the function from real-world data where the presence or absence of one or more future requests is known. The weights of the network are adjusted until the error on the training data is reduced to an acceptable level.

The backpropagation method is used to adjust the weights during training. The sigmoid and cross-entropy error functions are used as the activation function and objective function, respectively, for the neural network. The neural network has a single output which is interpreted as the probability that the object represented by the inputs is cacheable. NNPCR uses a two hidden layer structure since networks of this class are known to have a universal approximation property. Several sizes and hidden layer configurations were trained in an effort to find the smallest network possible. Networks which are too large often learn the training set well but are unable to generalize [1]. The hidden layers were usually kept at approximately the same size to ease training [1, 2]. The effects of these choices are discussed in Sect. 5.4.

The cache functions according to the behavior that Podlipnig et al. [3] suggest is typical of practical implementations; it caches all objects until it reaches a high mark (HM) and then selects objects for replacement until it reaches a low mark L. Network inputs represent recency, frequency, and size. Objects are selected for replacement according to the neural network's output; those with the lowest probability of being cacheable are replaced first. This approach is a function-based replacement strategy. Neural networks are often used to approximate functions from a sample of the data set [1]. The network is trained with requests from an hour-long segment of a trace file. A second hour-long segment is taken from a trace file for a different day in the same week. The second set is used as a verification set. The weights of the network are not adjusted based on the verification set, but the verification patterns are run across the network each epoch to measure how well the network is able to generalize the function.

NNPCR creates a neural network with small random weights in the range $\left[-\frac{1.1}{\sqrt{I}}, \frac{1.1}{\sqrt{I}}\right]$, where I is the number of inputs. The training cycle, or epoch, is repeated until the number of epochs reaches the maximum. Each pattern in the training set is applied to the neural network, and the derivatives are back-propagated based on a target output of 0 for uncacheable requests and 1 for cacheable requests. NNPCR records the error, and whether or not the request was classified correctly. A request is classified as cacheable if and only if the neural network output is greater than 0.5. The current set of error derivatives are added to the set

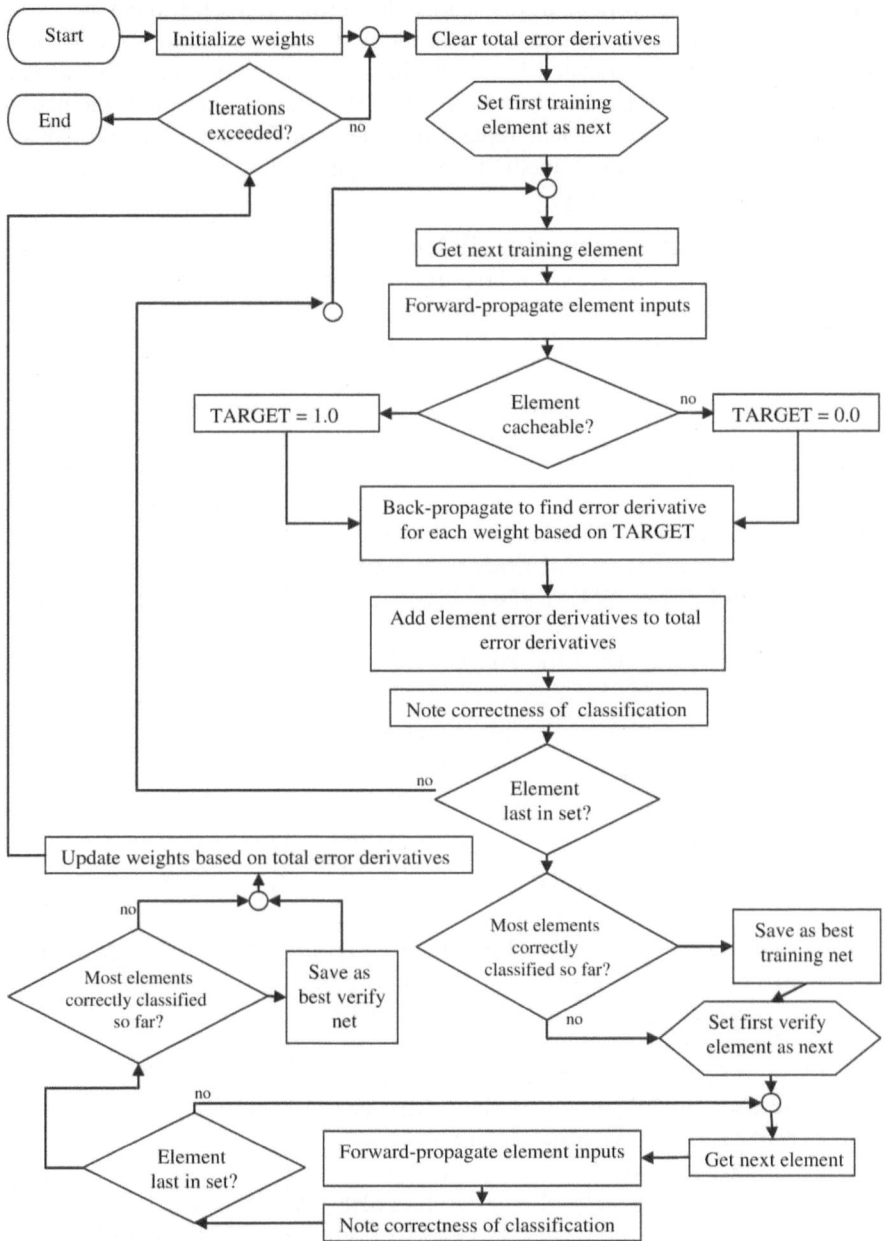

Fig. 5.1 NNPCR training process

of total error derivatives. At the end of each epoch, if the percentage of correctly classified training patterns are the highest seen so far in the training session, the network is saved to a file. To ensure good generalization, NNPCR also calculates the CCR the neural network achieves against the verification set. If this ratio is the highest seen so far in the training session, the network is saved to a second file. Finally, the weights are updated based on the set of total error derivatives. The following pseudo-code demonstrates how NNPCR constructs and trains the neural network employed in proxy cache replacement decisions assuming the previously mentioned high and low mark method is used. Figure 5.1 depicts the process as a flowchart for additional clarity.

```
neural_network* nnpcr_gen(int hidden_layers, int[] nodes,
                          int update_mode, int max_epochs,
                          trace_set training_set,
                          trace_set verify_set)
{
  neural_net = neural_network(hidden_layers + 2,nodes);
  initialize neural_net weights with small random values;
  iterations = 0;
/*
 /total_edw is a 3-dimensional array, indexed by layer and
 /sending and receiving nodes, in that order. For example,
 /total_edw[1][2][0] refers to the weighted connection
from
 /the third node in the first hidden layer (second actual
 layer)
 /to the first node in the second hidden layer.
 */
do
{
    set all values of total_edw array to 0;
    for(i = 0;i < length(training_set);i ++)
    {
      neural_net.forward_prop(training_set[i].inputs);
      if(training_set[i].is_cachable)
         neural_net.back_prop(1.0);
      else
         neural_net.back_prop(0.0);
      edw = neural_net.error_derivatives();
      for(j = 0; j < edw.depth; j ++)
         for(k = 0; k < edw.width; k ++)
            for(l = 0; l < edw.height; l ++)
               total_edw[j][k][l] += edw[j][k][l];
}
if(most training patterns classified so far)
   neural_net.save(best_training_net_file);
for(i = 0; i < length(verify_set); i ++)
   record number correctly classified;
```

```
if(most verification patterns classified so far)
   neural_net.save(best_verify_net_file);
neural_net.update_weights(total_edw);
   iterations ++;
} while(iterations < MAX_ITERATIONS);
return &neural_net;
}
```

NNPCR does not dictate exactly when replacement should occur, although training set simulation follows the high/low mark method from [3]. Once the cache is ready to replace one or more objects, NNPCR rates each candidate replacement object by applying each object's characteristics across the inputs of the neural network. NNPCR is flexible about the choice of characteristics but requires the characteristics used in application to match those used in training in terms of both format and semantics. The neural network's output is used as a replacement rating for the object. A lower score represents a better choice for replacement; one or more objects are selected for replacement using these ratings.

5.3 Simulation

Simulation consists of a simple iterative analysis procedure. Since this research is investigating the web proxy cache replacement problem as it exists independent of specific hardware, low-level cache simulation, such as that performed by DiskSim [4], is not necessary. The difference in time required to retrieve an object from the disk versus main memory is assumed to be trivial compared with the difference in time required to send an object from the cache versus retrieving and retransmitting a fresh copy of the object. The simulation ran with trace data from IRCache [5]. Unique documents were identified by size and uniform resource identifier (URI).

Rhea et al. [6] propose value-based web caching to address concerns about the effects of resource modification and aliasing. Although the point is valid, it is not considered by NNPCR because the actual data transmitted were not available. Furthermore, the trace data are sanitized before being made publicly available so that dynamic information is not available. For example, form data passed by appending the parameters to the URI are removed during sanitation. Finally, such approaches are designed with cache consistency in mind, which is beyond the scope of NNPCR.

5.3.1 Data Preprocessing

A significant amount of data preprocessing was needed to train the neural network. The IRCache trace files each covers one day and contains tens of thousands of requests. First, we used exhaustive search to convert each log file entry into an entry containing the URI, frequency, size, timestamp, and number of future requests for that day. Next, we eliminated internal Squid requests and generated recency values. Recency values were generated by running a cache simulation using the high/low water mark method discussed earlier. The timestamp of the most recently added or updated request was used as the current time. Lines were written out whenever a request was removed from the cache or caused a cache hit. Items were assigned a rating equal to the number of future requests for that item and replaced starting with the lowest rated. This process created log files with only the desired information and thus made them suitable for training. However, the log files were still excessive in length so one hour of the January 11, 2006 pa.us.ircache.net trace file was selected as the training set. One hour of the January 10, 2006 pa.us.ircache.net trace file was designated as the verification set. pa.us.ircache.net is located in Palo Alto, California. One should note that the information, such as future requests, in the hour-long sets reflected knowledge of the entire day, not just the particular hour. Finally, the inputs were normalized into the range [−0.9–0.9] to prevent node saturation. This was accomplished by tracking the maximum and minimum values of each property and then applying the following linear normalization function:

$$x_{norm} = \frac{x_{actual} - min_{data}}{max_{data} - min_{data}} \left(max_{tgt} \right) + min_{tgt} \tag{5.1}$$

5.3.2 Metrics

Hit rate and byte-hit rate are the two most commonly used metrics to evaluate the performance of cache replacement techniques [3, 7–9]. Podlipnig et al. [3] also mention the delay-savings ratio but claim it is unstable and thus not generally used. Hit rate refers to the ratio of objects served from the proxy cache versus those retrieved from the original server. This metric targets user perceived delay and availability. Byte-hit rate is the ratio of number of bytes served from the proxy cache versus retrieved from the original server. Optimizing for this metric reduces the amount of network traffic and thus eases link congestion. Algorithms that favor many small objects in the cache optimize for hit rate, whereas those that prefer fewer large objects optimize for byte-hit rate. In [3], an algorithm is considered "good enough" for current web proxy caching needs if it performs well for more than one metric. Therefore, both hit rate and byte-hit rate will be considered in evaluating NNPCR.

For training the network, the most important metric is the CCR. We use a combination of sigmoid activation units and the cross-entropy error function to interpret network output as the probability that a particular pattern represents a request in the cacheable class. A network output of 0.75 generates an error signal when the target is 1.0. However, since any network output >0.5 means the pattern is more likely cacheable than not, this pattern would still be classified correctly. Therefore, CCR is the criteria used for training purposes, while hit rate and byte-hit rate are the criteria for performance evaluation once training is considered complete.

5.3.3 Performance Evaluation

In order to judge how well the neural network performs, it is compared with LRU and LFU. Additionally, the neural network's performance is compared with a "perfect" function (optimal) which always rates an object with the number of future requests. LRU and LFU are used for comparison because they form the basis of current web proxy cache replacement algorithms. Our neural networks, like most current algorithms, use both frequency and recency to determine the likelihood of a future request. Comparing with LRU and LFU allows us to investigate the contributions of each of these factors to replacement performance separately and to see how our neural networks model the relationship between the two. We compare with the optimal algorithm to measure how well the neural networks perform relative to how well it is possible to perform. All cache replacement algorithms are attempting to predict future requests, if any, for the cache objects. Since we are evaluating performance in simulation using trace logs from a proxy server, we are able to compare with an algorithm that has absolute knowledge of the number of future requests. Thus, the optimal algorithm is the perfect HM for assessing the success of our technique.

The relationship between the CCR of the training set and that of the verification set is used to measure the neural network's ability to generalize. A high CCR on the training set coupled with a low ratio on the verification indicates that the neural network has become overtrained and does not generalize well.

5.4 Results

Several networks were trained with varying structure, learning rates (LRs), momentum rates (MRs), and choice of inputs. Batch-mode learning was used for all networks. The majority of the networks converged to the same classification maxima. Online-mode learning was also experimented with but did not result in convergence for any networks within a reasonable number of epoch equivalents. Successful convergence is heavily dependant upon how representative our training data is of the function we seek to approximate. The representativeness of any given point in our training set is questionable compared with the representativeness of the entire set, yet each weight update in online mode is based on a single data point. The maximum CCR for the training set and verification set was approximately 0.88. The impact of variations in LR and MR, excluding extreme values, was minimal compared with structural variation. Neural network structure is denoted such that *a/b/c/d* means the network has *a* inputs, *b* nodes in the first hidden layer, *c* nodes in the second hidden layer, and *d* output nodes.

The rest of the section is organized as follows. Section 5.4.1 analyzes the training of the neural networks. The change in CCR over weight adjustments (epochs) is shown for a variety of network structures. LR and MR values of 0.01 and 0.4, respectively, are used throughout the section. Variation in these values is not presented as the influence on training success was small; LR and MR values are provided for a sense of the magnitude of appropriate choices. The results of the cache simulation are shown in Sect. 5.4.2. A number of different neural network structures converged successfully during training; these networks are compared with LRU, LFU, and the optimal algorithm and one another in terms of the two major cache performance metrics: hit rate and byte-hit rate. In order to simulate a proxy cache, it was necessary to choose values for the high and low marks discussed earlier. The simulation results cover a range of choices for these values. Section 5.4.3 presents an analysis of the input/output mappings of the individual neural networks. Changes in the cacheable probability given by the respective neural networks in response to changing object information are examined, and the decision-making strategies developed during training are characterized. Finally, Sect. 5.4.4 discusses the practical application of this technique for system administrators.

5.4.1 Training

Figures 5.2 and 5.3 show the CCR for several different network structures over the first 200 epochs for the training set and verification set, respectively. Figures 5.4

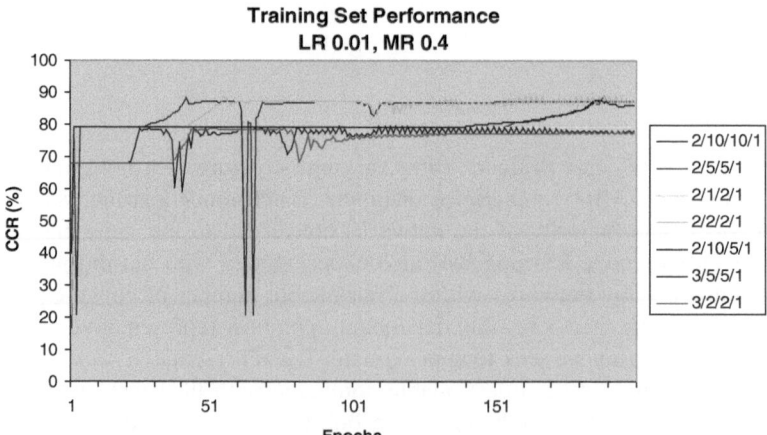

Fig. 5.2 Training set performance over 200 epochs

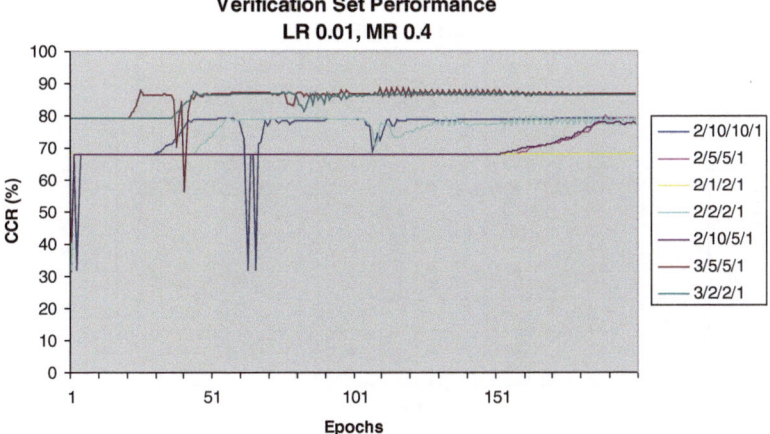

Fig. 5.3 Verification set performance over 200 epochs

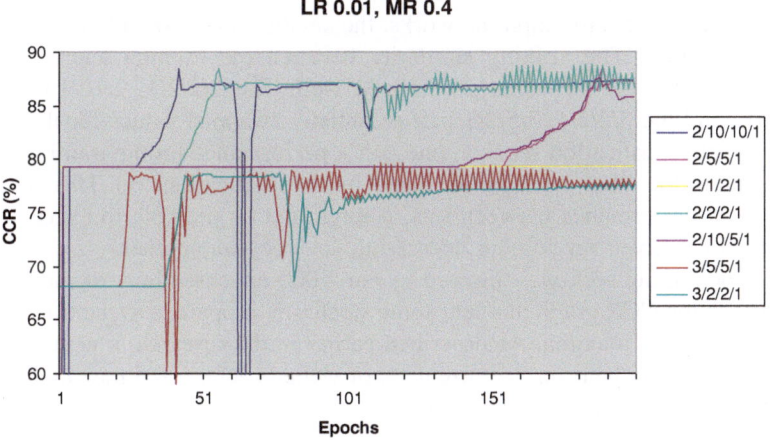

Fig. 5.4 Training set performance over 200 epochs for $60 < CCR < 90$

and 5.5 show a more detailed look at training behavior by ignoring the brief negative spikes in the CCR values of some networks.

These networks were initialized with different random weights. All the networks used frequency and recency as the first and second inputs, respectively. Neural networks with a hidden layer containing only a single node remained frozen after initialization and were unable to adjust, although lucky initializations sometimes started the networks at fairly high ratios. The smallest structure that was able to learn effectively through backpropagation was a 2/2/2/1 neural network. In fact, it frequently outperformed larger structures, such as 2/5/5/1, on both the training and verification data sets. This is a very encouraging result because

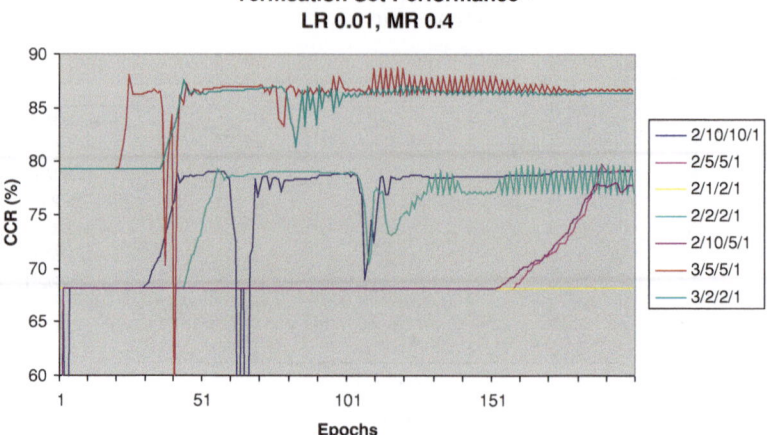

Fig. 5.5 Verification set performance over 200 epochs for $60 < CCR < 90$

these small networks are fast to train. Adding size as a third input yielded very similar results. For three-input networks, the smallest network able to learn was a 3/2/2/1 structure. The striking similarity between the training and verification graphs indicates the networks generalized well. The 2/2/2/1, 2/10/10/1 pair of networks and the 3/2/2/1, 3/5/5/1 pair essentially swapped values for the training set versus the verification set (i.e., one pair's performance on the training set was equivalent to the other pair's performance on the verification set). This suggests a trade-off in performance between sets; it might not be possible to exceed certain accuracy on a given set without decreasing accuracy on another.

Each neural network was allowed to run 2,000 epochs. Many of the networks had jitter in the CCR graph that lent some stochastic properties to the training once it approached the maxima. As described earlier in the research, a neural network was saved to file whenever its current set of weights achieved a new highest CCR for either the training or verification set.

5.4.2 Proxy Cache Simulation

Cache simulation was carried out on the entire January 16, 2006 trace file from pa.us.ircache.net. The cache size was set at 0.5 GB. Several combinations of high and low mark values were evaluated. The simulation was repeated for the optimal algorithm, LRU, LFU, and five different structures of neural network. For each structure, two neural networks were tested: (1) the network saved for best performance on the training set and (2) the network saved for the best performance on the verification set. For a HM of 0.2 GB, the 3/2/2/1 verification (V) network achieved the highest hit rates of the neural networks and both 2/2/2/1 networks

Table 5.1 Hit rates for a high mark of 0.2 GB and several low mark values

	LM: 0.001 (%)	LM: 0.01 (%)	LM: 0.05 (%)	LM: 0.1 (%)
Optimal	25.99	25.99	26.35	26.35
LRU	23.17	23.17	23.69	24.13
LFU	23.60	23.60	24.88	25.11
3/2/2/1	24.04	24.04	24.90	25.66
2/2/2/1	22.84	22.84	22.82	22.88

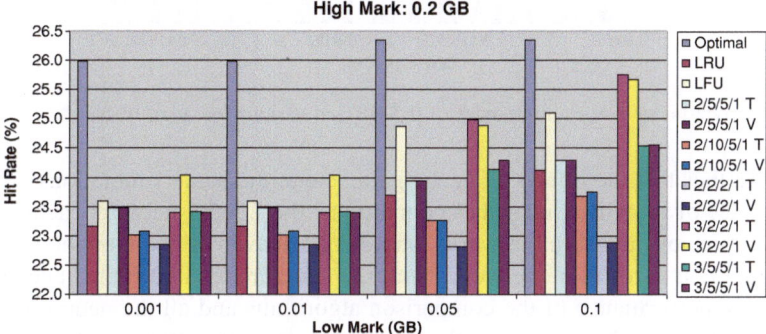

Fig. 5.6 Hit rates for the algorithms and neural networks for HM = 0.2 GB

shared the worst hit rates of the networks. Table 5.1 shows the hit rates of the optimal algorithm, LRU, LFU, the 3/2/2/1 verification network, and the 2/2/2/1 networks for a HM of 0.2 GB and various low mark (LM) values. Figure 5.6 illustrates the hit rate performance of all tested algorithms and neural networks for these same parameters.

Although the 3/2/2/1 verification network performed very well for the hit rate metric, it did the opposite for byte-hit rate. The 2/5/5/1 training (T) network had the highest byte-hit rates of the neural networks, but was the same or slightly worse than LFU. Table 5.2 shows some selected byte-hit rates, and Fig. 5.7 shows all the tested byte-hit rates for a HM of 0.2 GB.

Superior performance for the hit rate metric versus the byte-hit rate metric may be the result of training for classification only and not in terms of a size-related cost.

Table 5.2 Byte-hit rates for various low mark values and a high mark of 0.2 GB

	LM: 0.001 (%)	LM: 0.01 (%)	LM: 0.05 (%)	LM: 0.1 (%)
Optimal	25.61	25.61	26.20	26.20
LRU	24.00	24.00	24.26	24.65
LFU	24.54	24.54	24.69	24.88
3/2/2/1	24.09	24.09	24.00	23.92
2/5/5/1	24.54	24.54	24.46	24.68

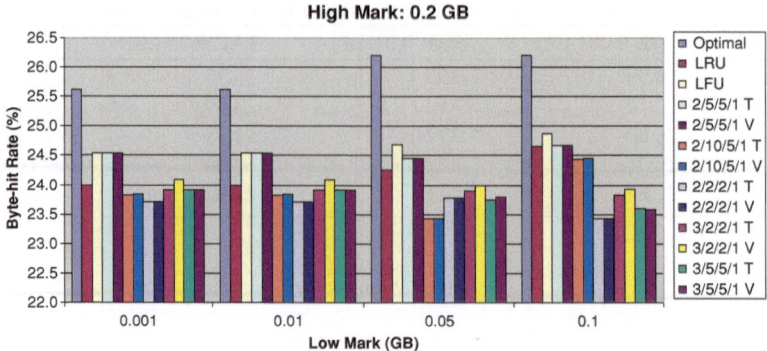

Fig. 5.7 Byte-hit rates for a high mark of 0.2 GB and various low mark values

To further test the effects of cache parameters, the same simulations were run with a HM of 0.4 GB. Under these conditions, the 2/5/5/1 networks achieved the best hit rates of the neural networks, and 2/2/2/1 networks had the worst hit rates. Table 5.3 compares these networks with the comparison algorithms, and Fig. 5.8 shows the performance of the comparison algorithms and all the neural networks.

For a 0.001 GB low mark, the networks and algorithms perform roughly equivalent. This results from the tight constraint of the small low mark value and the large gap between the high and low mark values. The low mark determines

Table 5.3 Algorithm and neural network hit rates for a high mark of 0.4 GB

	LM: 0.001 (%)	LM: 0.01 (%)	LM: 0.05 (%)	LM: 0.1 (%)
Optimal	24.78	25.93	26.35	26.35
LRU	24.68	24.84	25.19	25.36
LFU	24.73	25.05	25.61	25.79
2/5/5/1	24.78	24.98	25.29	25.41
2/2/2/1	24.69	24.70	24.78	24.89

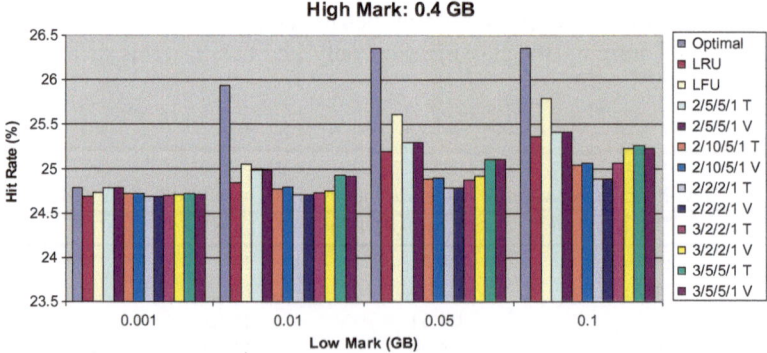

Fig. 5.8 Algorithm and neural network hit rates for a high mark of 0.4 GB

how much is left in the cache after a replacement, so at some point, it becomes low enough that not all cacheable requests can be stored at once. This effect is, of course, amplified by poor decisions that leave uncacheable requests in the cache. When the gap between the high and low mark values is large, the number of items that must be replaced in a single replacement increases. Furthermore, replacements are carried out less frequently, and thus, the algorithm or neural network responsible for replacement decisions does not evaluate the status of items in the cache as often. This can be problematic when, for example, many cacheable items are kept during a single replacement sweep but then receive their respective last accesses well before the HM is reached. Finally, infrequent replacement increases the performance cost of bad replacement decisions because of the additional time, selected requests are left untouched in the cache. As the low mark increases, LFU consistently has the high hit rate after the optimal algorithm. The 2/5/5/1 network trails LFU for low marks greater than 0.001 GB, but achieves a better hit rate than LRU for every low mark value. Byte-hit rates for the neural networks were consistent with the hit rate rankings; the 2/5/5/1 and 2/2/2/1 networks had the highest and lowest byte-hit rates, respectively. Table 5.4 compares these two networks with the other algorithms, and Fig. 5.9 shows byte-hit rates for the algorithms and all the neural networks.

The byte-hit rates were subject to the same constraint as hit rates for a low mark of 0.001 GB. In fact, this was the only case where the optimal algorithm did not

Table 5.4 Byte-hit rates for the algorithms and neural networks with a high mark of 0.4 GB

	LM: 0.001 (%)	LM: 0.01 (%)	LM: 0.05 (%)	LM: 0.1 (%)
Optimal	25.00	26.04	26.20	26.20
LRU	25.04	25.21	25.67	25.71
LFU	25.02	25.38	25.58	25.83
2/5/5/1	25.03	25.57	25.70	25.73
2/2/2/1	24.98	24.99	25.00	25.06

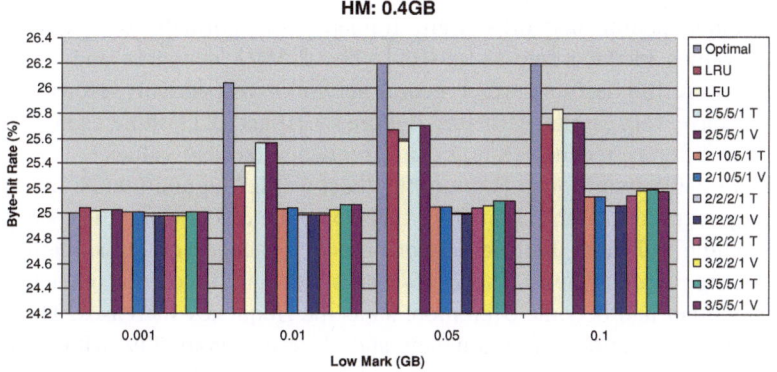

Fig. 5.9 Byte-hit rates for the algorithms and neural networks with a high mark of 0.4 GB

achieve the highest metric. However, this is an intuitive result since the optimal algorithm only considers the number of future requests and not the size of a request for replacement decisions. The 2/5/5/1 network performed very well for this metric; it had the highest byte-hit rates after the optimal for 2 of 3 low mark values greater than 0.001. LFU had a higher byte-hit rate when the low mark was 0.1 GB, but the magnitude of the difference between LFU and the 2/5/5/1 network for these parameters was small in comparison with the difference for a low mark of 0.01 GB.

5.4.3 Neural Network Input/Output Relationships

The proxy cache simulation results show that the neural networks are able to make competitive replacement decisions. Although no neural network fell behind the optimal algorithm by more than 2 % points, the local performance variation was significant. Additionally, changing cache parameters had a strong impact on individual neural network performance. In order to better understand the results presented earlier, an attempt was made to determine the characteristics of the individual networks that factor into proxy cache replacement performance.

We first note that the CCR used to measure training and generalization success did not predict the level of success in the simulation. The 2/2/2/1 networks had some of the highest CCR values on the training set, but performed the worst in simulation for all but one case. The 2/5/5/1 networks were relatively close to the 2/2/2/1 networks in CCR for both the training and verification sets, albeit slightly slower to converge, yet had the best overall performance of any of the neural networks. Since neural networks approximate functions from points of data, there are numerous functions the given network might approximate which are all best-fit for that data. In this application, the function is unknown, so the accuracy of a given network depends on how well its internal function matches the unknown function, not just the data points. The rest of this section explores the input-to-output mapping of the neural networks.

Two-input neural networks were trained with normalized frequency and recency values in the range [−0.9–0.9]. The 2/5/5/1 networks and the 2/2/2/1 networks were the best and worse neural networks, respectively. However, these networks have very similar structure. Figures 5.10 and 5.11 show each network's output for different recency (x-axis) and frequency (series) values.

The 2/2/2/1 network outputs resemble "backwards" sigmoid units. Increases in frequency seem to shift the sigmoid further down the recency axis. The steep slope in the middle indicates that the network quickly changes its classifications with subtle changes in the input. The 2/5/5/1 network outputs, on the other hand, are much smoother and become even more so as the frequency increases. The 2/5/5/1 outputs give preference to frequency and decrease gradually with increasing recency values (i.e., more time since the last access). Furthermore, as the frequency increases, the rate at which increased recency lowers the output is

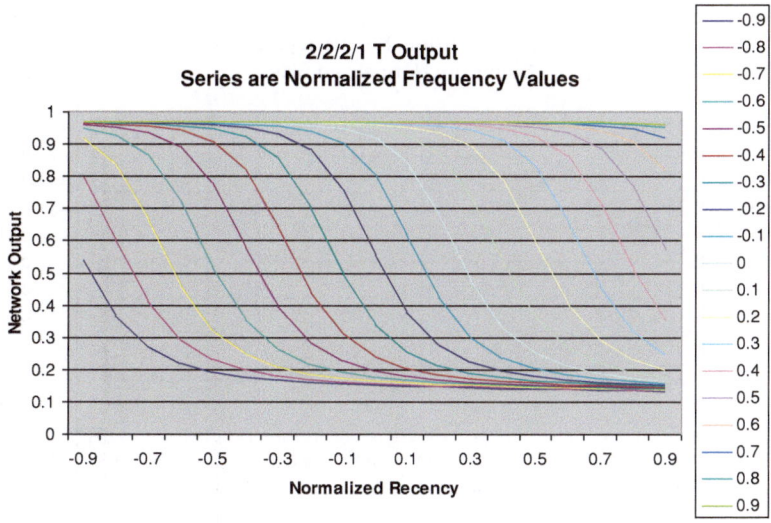

Fig. 5.10 Frequency and recency to network output for the 2/2/2/1 network

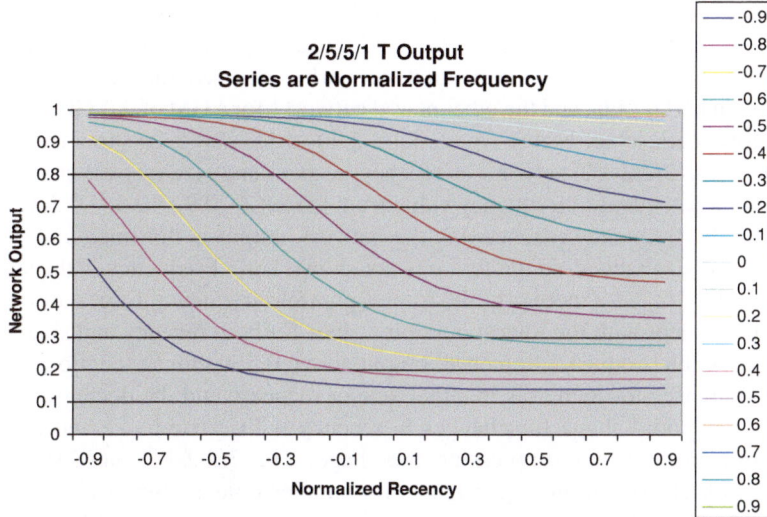

Fig. 5.11 Frequency and recency to network output for the 2/5/5/1 network

reduced. In other words, the 2/5/5/1 network has a more "intelligent" approach than the 2/2/2/1 network. The 2/2/2/1 network grasps the inverse relationship but models it crudely; for many frequency values, the output has a long tail with little output change as recency increases followed by a sharp drop to low output. In contrast, the 2/5/5/1 network's behavior is similar to LFU with an aging factor.

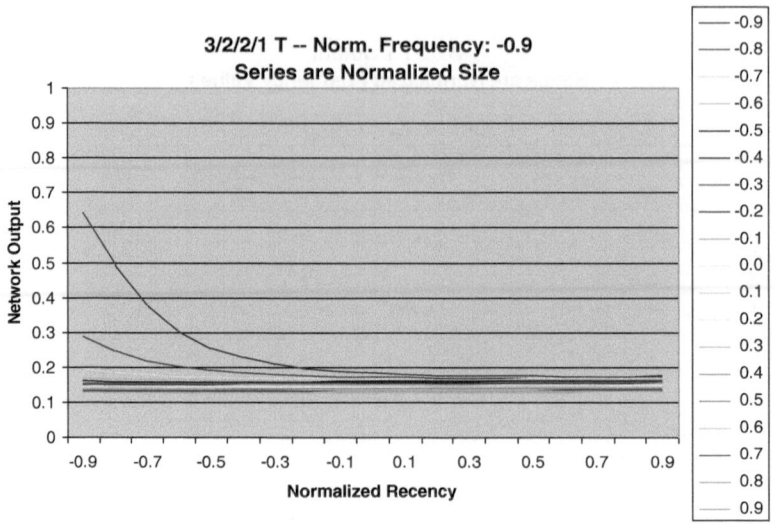

Fig. 5.12 3/2/2/1 T output for changing recency and size with a frequency of −0.9

Three-input networks used a normalized size value for the third input. Usually, the 3/2/2/1 and 3/5/5/1 networks did not stand out during simulation, but the 3/2/2/1 networks, particularly the verification network, achieved hit rates significantly higher than LRU, LFU, and the other neural networks for a HM of 0.2 GB, regardless of the low mark level. Figures 5.12, 5.13, 5.14, 5.15, and 5.16 show the network output for the 3/2/2/1 T network as recency (x-axis) and size (series) change; each figure is for a sequential frequency value from the set {−0.9, −0.6, −0.2, 0.2, 0.6}.

When the frequency reaches 0.9, the network output is flat-lined at 1.0 for all recency and size values, so the figure is not shown here. Frequency is the strongest factor in the 3/2/2/1 T network; the lowest possible frequency forces all output to below 0.5 except with the lowest possible values for both recency and size, and the highest possible frequency forces all output above 0.5 without exception. Network output decreases for increases in either size or recency, and the decrease in output follows a sigmoid shape for changes in recency with a fixed size and frequency when frequency is not suppressing the shape. The 3/2/2/1 T network is more lenient with classification requirements for smaller objects. Small objects require less frequency and more recency to be considered uncacheable than larger objects. However, the network shifts considerably from size to recency suddenly in a manner similar to the 2/2/2/1 network.

To summarize, the 2/2/2/1 network had the worst performance. It was characterized by balanced weighting of frequency and recency but with outputs tending toward extreme high or low values with a sudden classification shift between the two. The network's decision making is weak because the output is heavily clustered around 0.0 and 1.0; thus, little to no distinction is made between items on one of the tails of the sigmoid. The 2/5/5/1 network had the best overall performance.

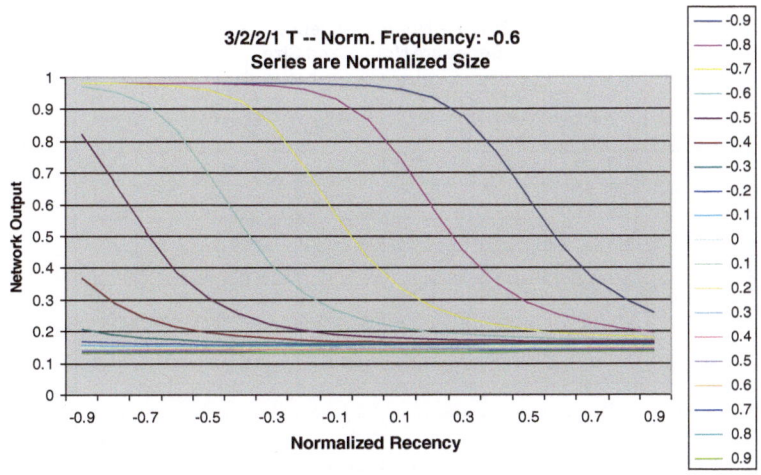

Fig. 5.13 3/2/2/1 output for changing recency and size with a frequency of −0.6

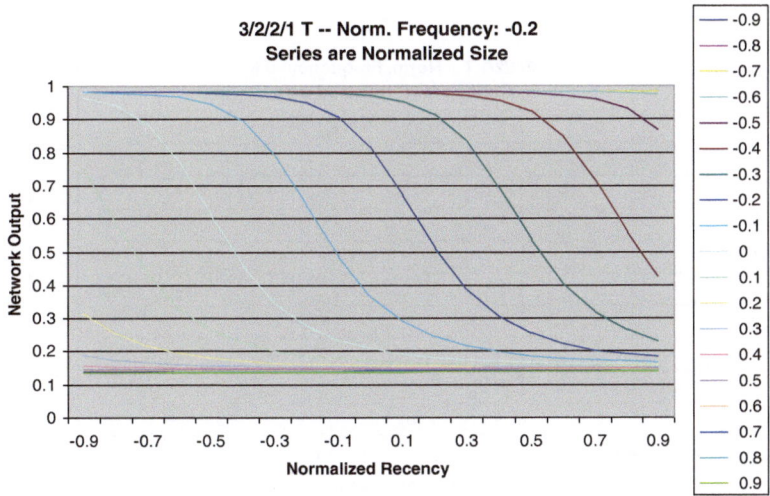

Fig. 5.14 3/2/2/1 T output for changing recency and size with a frequency of −0.2

It was characterized by considering frequency foremost with recency used as an aging factor. Additionally, the rate of change due to recency decreased with increasing frequency. The 2/5/5/1 network's performance may be attributed to its additional subtly in mapping input to output. It does not have the same loss of distinction due to extended tails as the 2/2/2/1 network. Also, the change in output as recency changes assumes different shapes for different frequency values rather than simply shifting the points of inflection. Finally, the 3/2/2/1 network was generally unremarkable but excelled for hit rate with a HM of 0.2 GB. It was characterized by the use of frequency as the overriding factor and a preference for

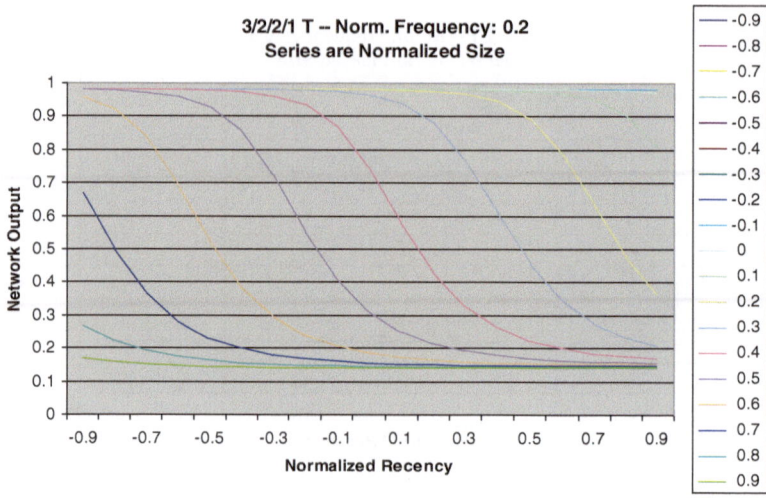

Fig. 5.15 3/2/2/1 T output for changing recency and size with a frequency of 0.2

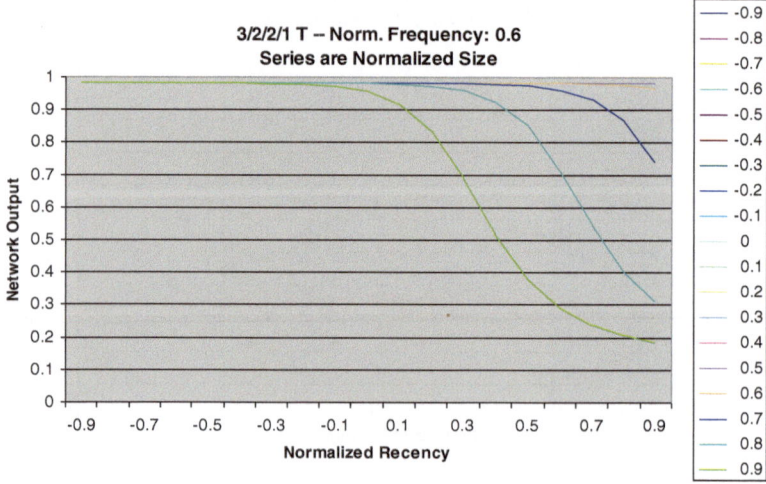

Fig. 5.16 3/2/2/1 T output for changing recency and size with a frequency of 0.6

classifying small objects as cacheable. The output was heavily clustered in a manner similar to the 2/2/2/1 network. The 3/2/2/1 network targets hit rate over byte-hit rate by virtue of its size consideration; choosing many small items attempts to maximize hit rate, whereas choosing fewer large items attempts to maximize byte-hit rate. The network likely suffers from clustering problems similar to the 2/2/2/1 network, but may gain an advantage for lower HMs because it will not "plug" the cache with a very large object.

5.4.4 Application

This research is a proof of concept for the application of neural networks to web proxy cache replacement. Although some aspects of this technique require context-specific choices on the part of the system administrator, a number of parameters are fixed. The neural networks should follow the MLP model; they should be feed-forward, layered, and fully connected between layers. The neural network structure should consist of one input layer, two hidden layers, and one output layer. The input layer should have either two nodes or three nodes. The nodes should be given normalized values, respectively, representing recency, frequency, and, in the case where three nodes are used, size. The output layer should have only one node, and its value should be interpreted as the probability that the object being evaluated is cacheable. The sigmoid function should be used as the node activation function. Neural network weights should be set via training using batch-mode backpropagation. The error function used for training should be the cross-entropy error function. Training success should be measured with the CCR, and this metric should be applied to the training set and a verification set which the neural network has not trained against. Table 5.5 summarizes NNPCR's fixed parameters.

System administrators will have to make some individualized decisions regarding the parameters used for constructing the neural network in order to apply this technique. We found that neural networks can train successfully for this function with a variety of parameter choices. Although these choices affect performance, it is not possible to give exact values for the general case. We presented results for training with a LR and MR of 0.01 and 0.4, respectively. These are reasonable starting points; however, system administrators should be aware that the shape of the error surface is unknown. Furthermore, they should keep in mind that the weights are initialized randomly, so the initial location on the error surface is also unknown. Table 5.6 provides a list of variable parameters and suggested value ranges.

The number of epochs allowed for training each individual neural network should be adapted by the system administrator. The number of epochs allowed is a

Table 5.5 NNPCR fixed parameters

Parameter	Value
Neural network model	Fully connected, feed-forward MLP model
Hidden layers	2
Normalized input range	$[-0.9, 0.9]$
Activation function	Sigmoid
Error function	Cross-entropy error
Inputs	2 (recency, frequency) or 3 (recency, frequency, and size)
Outputs	1 (likelihood of a future request)
Weight update algorithm	Batch-mode backpropagation
Training metric	Correct classification ratio

Table 5.6 NNPCR variable parameters

Parameter	Suggested value(s)
Learning rate	0.005–0.05
Momentum rate	0.2–0.6
Nodes per hidden layer	3–10
Training epochs allowed	500–2000

very heavy factor in determining the total computational cost of applying this technique. By saving the neural network after any epoch in which it has achieved the highest CCR of the training run, NNPCR assures that the administrator has the best weight set possible for the time put into training. For our own results, we allowed 2,000 epochs for each neural network, yet all of our successful networks had CCRs very close to their respective maximums within a couple hundred epochs. Allowing additional training epochs for a neural network that has already converged always has the possibility of achieving a weight set with a better CCR, but there are diminishing returns as the number of epoch increases. On the other hand, the administrator should abort training early for a new neural network that shows little or no change in CCR during the early training epochs. In this research, the neural networks which exhibited this behavior—those with only a single node in either hidden layer—were unable to train successfully.

The last decision required of the system administrator is the number of structural variations that will be trained and which specific structures they will be. The computational cost of a given network is directly determined by its size; the most expensive operation for using a neural network in proxy cache replacement is the activation function, which is evaluated once per node per cache object rated. However, a larger structure provides increased flexibility in the input-to-output mapping which can increase the performance. Since individual network performance is both data and cache parameter dependant, the administrator should train multiple networks and select one for use based on size versus performance under cache parameters similar, if not identical, to those of the target proxy cache. In addition to the data set, the expected workload profile of the proxy cache should be accounted for in the structure of the neural network. Under a heavy workload, fewer hidden nodes are preferable because objects need to be evaluated more frequently. On the other hand, a light workload can support larger numbers of hidden nodes and greater nuance in the resulting neural network decision structure.

5.5 Summary and Conclusions

A number of algorithms for web proxy cache replacement appear in the literature. Although most are based on strategies used in local disk caching, such as LRU and LFU, algorithms have been developed for web proxy caches specifically because the traffic patterns seen by a web proxy server vary from those seen in local caches on significant characteristics such as variation in object size and locality of references. The respective performances of the replacement algorithms are heavily dependant on metric and workload. These algorithms tend to either have assumptions about workload characteristics built in or include tunable parameters to control which assumption(s) the algorithm favors.

MLP model neural networks use layered nodes with weighted connections to approximate continuous functions. MLP model neural networks are appropriate for web proxy caching because they are able to learn by example and generalize knowledge gained through training. The weights can be set to appropriate values through the process of supervised learning, wherein the network is trained against known input/output pairs and the weights are adjusted accordingly until the network converges to presenting correct output for all patterns in the training set. If the network is not overtrained, it should then be able to generalize reasonably to patterns outside the training set.

NNPCR is a novel web proxy cache replacement scheme which incorporates a neural network. The network is a two hidden layer feed-forward artificial neural network which falls under the MLP model. NNPCR sets the connection weights through supervised learning with backpropagation. NNPCR trains the network using subsets of the trace data sets. Additionally, it uses separate subsets of the trace data sets for verification of network generalization. Error is calculated by using the known classification of each request for target output. Once the neural network has been created and properly trained, NNPCR is used to handle cache replacement decisions. All candidate replacement objects were rated either by applying frequency and recency information alone or by applying those parameters plus size, across the inputs of the network. An object is selected for replacement based on the rating returned by the neural network. NNPCR aims to take advantage of neural networks' universal approximation and generalization properties. The neural networks created by NNPCR were able to classify both training and verification sets with CCR values in the range of 0.85 to 0.88, which indicates effective generalization. NNPCR derives workload assumptions from the training data (partial workloads) rather than holding a static set of assumptions or requiring the user to set parameters that dictate which assumptions behavior will reflect.

In this chapter, we have demonstrated that a properly structured neural network can be efficiently trained to perform web proxy cache replacement from real-world data. Furthermore, we have shown that such a network is able to effectively generalize other workloads in a similar environment. We have presented simulation results which suggest this approach is a promising approach to web proxy cache replacement. Finally, we have explored the input–output mapping of several neural networks and identified characteristics of these mappings that are potential causes for weak versus strong performance.

The simulation results confirm our motivating hypothesis, which is that a general model of web proxy traffic can be derived bottom-up from samples of actual traffic. We showed that such a model can be represented by neural networks of small size, and that neural networks only slightly larger than the minimum trainable size demonstrated increased adaptivity in their respective decision mappings. This is important because it means this approach is flexible and allows trade-off between size and the complexity of the input-to-output mapping of a neural network, yet has very low minimum size, and therefore computational cost, requirements.

References

1. R. D. Reed, R. J. Marks II, *Neural smithing: supervised learning in feedforward artificial neural networks* (The MIT Press, Cambridge, 1999)
2. J. de Villiers, E. Barnard, Backpropagation neural nets with one and two hidden layers. IEEE Trans. Neural Networks **4**(1), 136–141 (1993)
3. S. Podlipnig, L. Böszörmenyi, A survey of web cache replacement strategies. ACM Comput. Surv. **35**(4), 374–398 (2003)
4. G. Ganger, B. Worthington, Y. Patt and J. Bucy, The DiskSim Simulation Environment (2005), [Online document] Available http://www.pml.cdu.edu/DiskSim/. Cited 16 Sept 2005
5. IRCache Home, [Online document] Available http://ircache.net/. Cited 5 Sept 2005
6. S. C. Rhea, K. Liang, E. Brewer, Value-based Web caching, in *Proceedings of the 12th International Conference on World Wide Web*, ACM Press, pp. 619–628 (2003)
7. M. Arlitt, L. Cherkasova, J. Dilley, R. Friedrich, T. Jin, Evaluating content management techniques for Web proxy caches. ACM SIGMETRICS Perform. Eval. Rev. **27**(4), 3–11 (2000)
8. R. Caceres, F. Douglis, A. Feldmann, G. Glass, M. Rabinovich, Web proxy caching: the devil is in the details. ACM SIGMETRICS Perform. Eval. Rev. **26**(3), 11–15 (1998)
9. L. Rizzo, L. Vicisano, Replacement policies for a proxy cache. IEEE/ACM Trans. Networking **8**(2), 158–170 (2000)

Chapter 6
Implementation of a Neural Network Proxy Cache Replacement Strategy in the Squid Proxy Server

Keywords NNPCR-2 · Neural network proxy cache replacement (NNPCR) · Web proxies · Proxy caching · Neural networks · Hit rate · Byte-hit rate · Trace file · IRCache · Squid · Sliding window · Hidden node · Learning rate

6.1 Introduction

This chapter presents the implementation of neural network proxy cache replacement (NNPCR) in a real environment, namely in the Squid proxy server. In order to do so, we propose an improved strategy of NNPCR referred to as NNPCR-2. We show how the improved model can be trained with up to 12 times more data and gain a 5–10 % increase in correct classification ratio (CCR) than in NNPCR. We implemented NNPCR-2 in Squid proxy server and compared it with four other cache replacement strategies. In this research, we use 84 times more data than NNPCR was tested against and present exhaustive test results for NNPCR-2 with different trace files and neural network structures. Our results demonstrate that NNPCR-2 made important, balanced decisions in relation to the hit rate and byte-hit rate; the two performance metrics most commonly used to measure the performance of web proxy caches.

The rest of this chapter is structured as follows. Section 6.2 describes current cache replacement strategies implemented in Squid. Section 6.3 discusses our improved implementation of NNPCR, known as NNPCR-2, its training, and lastly its implementation in Squid version 3.1. Our training results of NNPCR-2 are presented in Sect. 6.4, as well as the criteria for measuring the training performance. Section 6.5 describes the testing setup for Squid and how each strategy was benchmarked. Section 6.6 presents the results and observations of our tests of

H. ElAarag, *Web Proxy Cache Replacement Strategies*,
SpringerBriefs in Computer Science, DOI: 10.1007/978-1-4471-4893-7_6,
© Hala ElAarag 2013

various cache replacement strategies covered in this research including NNPCR-2. We conclude our results in Sect. 6.7.

6.2 Squid's Implemented Cache Replacement Strategies

Currently, Squid provides a choice between LFU dynamic-aging (LFU-DA) [1], Greedy-dual size/frequency (GDSF) [1], a heap-based variation of LRU, and by default enables a linked-list version of its LRU variant. The result from our tests shown later demonstrates that LRU, while a great base algorithm, in fact has a lower performance than LFU-DA and GDSF. GDSF also operates under a different *cost model* than our simulations presented in Chap. 4 and has unique effects on the algorithm. If the maximum size threshold for objects is increased, LFU-DA's performance can actually be changed as well.

Due to these recent developments, Squid is a good test bed for NNPCR. As the need for web proxy caching increases, Squid grows more popular in use and in support, and the added support and popularity have lead to a rather stable product. In fact, as early as 1999, Dilley et al. [2] from Hewlett Packard's Internet Systems and Applications Laboratory were responsible for adding LFU-DA and GDSF along with the heap-variation of LRU to Squid. Their research sheds light on how to go about implementing replacement policies for Squid and different configurations to test.

LFU-DA, GDSF, and LRU are implemented in Squid by using a general class known as the heap-based replacement strategy. Here, the assumption is to induce a total ordering to the current objects in the cache. Due to heap implementation, objects could be ordered based on a request value with a complexity of $O(nlog_2(n))$. Squid's heap replacement strategy is designed around callback functions (a strategy signified by pointing certain components or methods to functions responsible for giving the proper output); all one has to do is implement a new "key" generation callback function and allows Squid to be configured to point to that function. This will be covered later in more detail in the implementation section.

6.3 NNPCR-2

While simulations demonstrated that NNPCR would achieve high performance rates, there were several limitations we encountered in this research. NNPCR had a two-hour training set and then a two-hour testing set. More favorably training and testing should be for longer periods. In this way, we can ensure that NNPCR-2 would perform well for a long period of uptime.

More than anything else, the recency input is heavily related to the running time of the strategy. This even affects the target output for training the strategy. For instance, if an object has a mean time between requests of four hours, is it worth it to cache the object? According to NNPCR, each of these requests when trained by the neural network would have a target value of 1.0 despite the fact that the object would most likely expire from the cache well before.

NNPCR was also able to read in the trace files prior to running each training/ simulation session and found the maximum recency, frequency, and size values. This is clearly impossible in a running implementation. So clearly, we must define thresholds for each of the inputs and cap them if they happen to go above so that we can normalize our values into the input range [−0.9 to 0.9] still. However, by adding more parameters/thresholds, we now make NNPCR more parameterized than before, taking away from its dynamic characteristics. In the following sections, we will describe the new method of normalizing our inputs, as well as redefining our target value.

6.3.1 NNPCR-2 Implementation Details

In this section, we provide the details for our implementation of NNPCR-2 and the revisions we applied to the original NNPCR.

6.3.1.1 Input Normalization Methods and the Sliding Window

There are three inputs that NNPCR requires Recency, Frequency, and Size. Of the three, recency is the most troublesome of the parameters to normalize. Clearly, it is possible that the highest recency value could be up to a day, week, even more. However, it is unlikely that most objects will see a recency value that high, which means when we normalize our value, most objects will clutter around −0.9, which will not allow the neural network to be able to generalize very well. It may get to the point where the neural network would just concentrate on the other two inputs, namely frequency and size, respectively, and zero out the weights to the recency input node if it did not tell enough information. By zeroing out the weights, the neural network would have nullified the purpose of using recency as an indicator for cacheability.

To counter this issue, we decided to implement a sliding window around the time a request is made. With this in mind, we could train our neural network around this sliding window and redefine the semantic of our output value to go according to this sliding window. In NNPCR, we could say that the sliding window had a length of two hours, since all the testing and training were done within two hours. That means any output by the neural network was a judgment for within the next couple of hours.

To formally define what we mean by a sliding window, the system administrator would have to train and configure the neural network based on some sliding window length (SWL) generally set in milliseconds for our training program and seconds for Squid version 3.1. The sliding window of a request is thus the time before and after when the request was made. Within this sliding window, we can examine the frequency count during training and the recency time. As a general rule of thumb, the sliding window should be around the mean time that an object generally stays in a cache. From here on, the SWL will be referred to as SWL. Other symbols for object characteristics are shown in Table 4.2.

With the sliding window in mind, we update the recency value at each request to an object. When an object is requested, we set the recency value as shown in Eq. 6.1, which means that the recency value is set to the maximum of SWL and ΔT_i if object i was requested before, that is, ΔT_i is greater than 0. Otherwise, it will be set to SWL.

$$\text{recency}(x) = \max(\text{SWL}, \Delta T_i) \tag{6.1}$$

With this method, we then normalize the values into the range of $[-0.9 \text{ to } 0.9]$ by a typical linear normalization formula such as shown in Eq. 6.2. Where $\max_{\text{norm}} = 0.9$, $\min_{\text{norm}} = -0.9$, $\max_{\text{data}}$ and $\min_{\text{data}}$ are the maximum and minimum values in the data, respectively, x_{actual} is the value before normalization, while x_{norm} is the normalized value.

$$x_{\text{norm}} = \frac{x_{\text{actual}} - \min_{\text{data}}}{\max_{\text{data}} - \min_{\text{data}}} * \left(\max_{\text{norm}} - \min_{\text{norm}} \right) + \min_{\text{norm}} \tag{6.2}$$

For the frequency input value, it is relatively simple to decide on a threshold value. We must choose a frequency high enough that most objects will not ever reach it, but low enough so that the input values are dispersed evenly across the range $[-0.9 \text{ to } 0.9]$. In [5], we discussed how methods such as the cubic selection scheme (CSS) [3] and pyramidal selection scheme (PSS) [4] have a maximum frequency and size threshold to order objects into set classes. This method of choosing a frequency in conjunction with a size threshold value lead to some decent assumptions about various "classes" of objects based on their frequency and size class. As such, CSS and PSS perform quite well. We found that a maximum frequency of 128 was a good enough range [5]. Thus, in this research, we capped any frequency inputs to 128.

As stated before, CSS and PSS also incorporated *object classes* based on their size and their frequency as well. An object i belonged to a class j if and only if $j = \log(S_i + 1)$. For NNPCR-2, we decided to divide objects into their size classes as well, as opposed to capping the threshold. This was done in hopes of pushing the neural network to generalize based on objects within their size classes. We then had to add a threshold to the size classes instead of the maximum object size. Since the size class is a logarithmic scale, the neural network has the ability to realize precise relationships with objects at lower sizes; between 2 and 1024 bytes, there are 10 unique classes, while from 1024 to 2048, there are only 2 unique classes. This allows the neural networks to generalize about objects that are within class sizes, instead of specific sizes, which tends to be the case statistically as well. For this research, we chose a maximum size class of 22, which holds objects in the range $[2^{22}, 2^{23})$ bytes or up to 8 MB. Objects above 8 MB are essentially capped at that value and examined as if they were from the size 22 class.

6.3.1.2 Target Value and the Sliding Window

Now that we have set what the inputs will be for each pattern, we must now figure out what the neural network output will signify while still keeping it as some classification problem dealing with the likelihood of a future request. However, in order for the network output to signify anything, we must know what the target output value will be during the training process.

Building on the aforementioned sliding window on a particular request, the main method is to use the SWL of information in the past to make judgments on what will occur in the SWL ahead of the request. Since the previous section dealt with the sliding window prior to the request, then clearly the target value must deal with information following the request.

Semantically then the output node of the neural network must then represent the likelihood that a request occurs within the SWL *after* a request or particular pattern. Thus, simply, the target value of the neural network is 1.0 when there is in fact a request to the same object within the SWL afterward, and 0.0 otherwise. This is represented in Eq. 6.3.

$$\text{target}_p = \begin{cases} 1.0 & \text{if } \Delta T_i \leq \text{SWL}, \\ 0.0 & \text{otherwise} \end{cases} \tag{6.3}$$

Since the actual output of the neural network can also represent a probability, then anything that is above 0.5 can be classified as *cacheable* and anything below, as *unlikely cacheable within the SWL*. This is how we measure how the neural network correctly classifies a request. If we take the ratio of the number of patterns correctly classified as cacheable or unlikely cacheable to the total number of patterns, then we have the CCR.

6.3.1.3 Frequency Values and the Sliding Window Length

When training the neural network, we estimated how the frequency values might be represented in a functional cache; we did not want to continually keep incrementing the frequency counter because of how the neural network was being trained. Assume the case where based on the SWL, a target value of a particular request is set to 0. In an actual implementation of NNPCR-2, the corresponding object might be removed as a result, and thus, its frequency counter would be reset when it was removed from the cache. When it was seen again, its frequency counter would be reinitialized to 1.

Thus, we assume that if ΔT_i is less than SWL, then frequency of object x will be incremented by 1. Otherwise, the frequency count would be "decayed" by the number of sliding windows it is away from or set to 1, whichever is greater as shown in Eq. 6.4. Note that if a previous request did not occur before, then frequency(x) is set to 1.

$$
\text{frequency}(x) =
\begin{cases}
\text{frequency}(x) + 1 & \text{If } \Delta T_i \leq \text{SWL}, \\
\text{MAX}\left(\dfrac{\text{frequency}(x)}{\left\lceil \frac{\Delta T_i}{\text{SWL}} \right\rceil}, \; 1\right) & \text{otherwise}
\end{cases}
\tag{6.4}
$$

The reason for the frequency decaying factor is that if the previous request was outside SWL, then clearly the target value of that previous request would be 0.0, and thus, unlikely to remain in the cache (we assume that the expected value of the frequency count in this scenario is proportional to the number of sliding windows that separate the requests). Conversely, if the previous request was within SWL, then chances are, it would remain in the cache in the optimal cache setting, and thus the frequency information would be retained fully.

6.3.2 NNPCR-2 Training Setup

For training NNPCR-2, we used 3 different trace files provided to us by IRCache.net [6]. The trace files used for training spanned a day's worth of recorded web requests, which is a lot longer than the training time of NNPCR. We also cleaned the trace files prior to feeding them through the neural network, allowing the neural network to be trained only on requests that would actually be cached in a web server.

We implemented a training program for NNPCR-2 separate from Squid. The reason for this is that we did not need an actual functioning cache to train the neural network. Rather, we just needed to process patterns, feed them forward, and then back propagate the error.

The three locations of the trace files were Palo Alto, CA, New York, NY, and Urbana-Champaign, IL. They varied greatly in the number of requests and other request stream characteristics. The days that were used for each were arbitrarily chosen from the week of June 10 to 17, 2007, and used as the training sets. The idea here was to test how well a long-term configuration of a neural network might pervade and observe how well it may generalize information about the request streams. By having several different trainings of other trace files, we were also able to test whether particular configurations were affected by the training sets used.

For NNPCR-2, the training metric, same as NNPCR, is known as the CCR. CCR measures the number of patterns that the neural network correctly classifies (in this case, "cacheable" versus "unlikely cacheable"), to the total number of patterns seen in any given epoch.

We also followed the Pocket Algorithm [7], which saves the best weight set found during the testing procedure. This "best weight set" is measured by CCR. By saving this set throughout the training process, we can be assured that as time goes on, this best set will converge closer and closer to the global optimum. If we just used the last weight set at the end of the training, we may be using a weight set which was traversing an error plane and thus is not a good representation of what the neural network had learned in the past.

Another component of NNPCR-2's training, which differs greatly from NNPCR, is that we trained in online mode. When training in batch mode, we found that the values of CCR had huge discrepancies between consecutive epochs, which normally indicate that the learning rate (LR) is too high. Even turning down the learning and momentum rates, we were still unable to have the neural network stabilize to an acceptable CCR within 1500–2000 epochs. However, as we will show in Sect. 6.5, using online mode, we are able to easily have the network converge to an acceptable CCR within 500 epochs.

Lastly, one of the most important additions to NNPCR-2 is the inclusion of the bias node. Reed et al. [7] discuss how the absence of a bias node means the input pattern (0, 0 … 0) will always intercept at the origin, or rather all outputs will be 0. Even with multiple hidden layers, this problem is always inherited. However, if we include a bias node, a node which is set to some constant, typically 1.0, then we can overcome the problem. As a result, on top of the original 2 or 3 inputs, we also added another input node, which is always set to 1.0 in our neural network both in training and implementation.

6.3.3 Implementation of NNPCR-2 in Squid 3.1

The Squid implementation of NNPCR-2 has condensed the components of the neural network as much as possible—the only functionality that NNPCR-2 contains within Squid is that it can feed forward a pattern and produce an output but includes none of the training functions such as back-propagation, target outputs. We implemented the entire algorithm within its own class called NNPCR. The entire implementation was done in C/C ++, as that is the code base of Squid as well. Clearly, hard coding the sliding window length, size, and frequency thresholds, inputs, weights, etc., were not an option in a well-designed implementation; thus, we implemented a flat file loader to read in a particular *nnpcr_squid* formatted file. This file could be written simply in any text editor, or by utilizing our training program, which produces the files as output.

We made a major change to how the heap generated keys for objects it held. In Sect. 6.2, we alluded to how Squid uses callback functions to call what is known as the heap_key_gen_function. Since the output of the neural network can be interpreted as a request value of the object, then the only addition was to implement a new key generating function. However, the current implementation did not support being able to pass parameters other than the heap_age or object which the key was being generated for. As a result, we added a new parameter to this function, void *key_param, which allowed us to pass an instance of the NNPCR class (initialized at the Squid startup process with the flat file loader) transparently as a parameter to the key generation function, and without affecting the other replacement methods (since the key_param would just be null in those cases).

Interestingly, the heap_age parameter is saved and passed to all instances of this callback function. The heap_age is actually the aging factor required for both LFU-DA and GDSF. Thus, upon an object removal, despite whatever key generation function was used, heap_age is set to the removed object's key value.

One reason for this aging factor is to quickly expire objects that have not been requested in a while, solving the *cache pollution* problem that can be brought on by the cache replacement strategy. When we first tested NNPCR-2 in Squid, our first emulations demonstrated that there was cache pollution occurring. In NNPCR, the two-hour span did not have to worry about cache pollution, because if an object was requested within that time span, it was most likely going to be seen again during the testing or not have long enough time to become a pollutant. As we will cover later, our tests covered an entire week's worth of web requests—certainly enough time for many objects to become a pollutant. Since NNPCR and NNPCR-2 output a value in the range [0.0, 1.0], objects with high values in the beginning will stay in the cache until they either expire or outlast their benefit effectively polluting the cache. Thus, we had to implement an aging factor to the output of NNPCR's neural network. The heap_key_gen_function is only called when objects are added into the cache or upon a cache hit.

6.4 NNPCR Training Results

As mentioned earlier, we trained the neural networks based on three trace files, each covering a day of recorded requests, and each from three different locations. We tested the effects of altering the number of hidden nodes, input nodes, LR, and the SWL. We also tested altering the momentum rate, but it had such a small effect overall, that it was not worth reporting. Thus, for all our tests, the momentum rate (MR) was set to 0.2.

The results will be broken up based on the effects of altering certain factors for each of the trace files. The trace file from Palo Alto, California will be abbreviated as PA, New York, New York as NY, and Urbana-Champaign, Illinois as UC. Once cleansed, the PA training set had about 9,457 patterns, NY had about 157, 838 patterns, and lastly the UC had 248,542 patterns—all of them spanned an entire day's worth of recorded web requests.

We refer to neural networks by their standard convention, which is a neural network with two inputs, three hidden nodes in each of its two hidden layers, and then 1 output node would be labeled as a 2/3/3/1 network. Since we have added a bias node, however, keep in mind that this does affect the input count.

Lastly, we set all the tests to 1,000 epochs. This may seem like overkill, but some of the best patterns did end up showing up later toward 1,000 as well. One observation we did notice in all our tests is that the neural network always converges quickly and tends to stabilize within 100 epochs in online mode, which

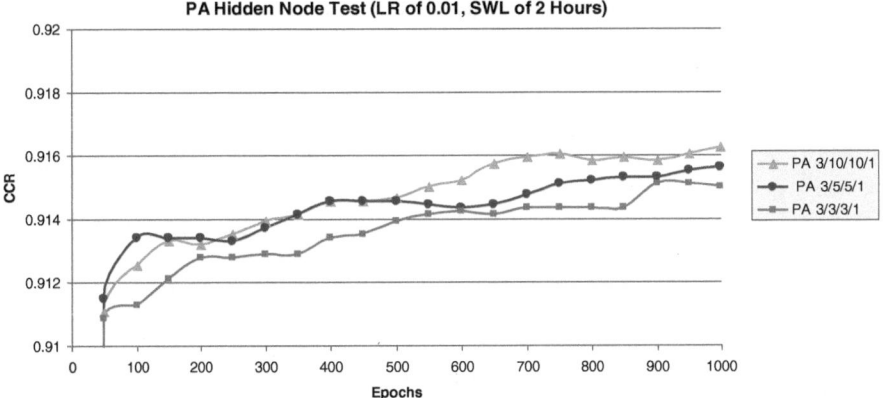

Fig. 6.1 Effect of hidden nodes for PA

means the error rate will continually keep decreasing at a steady rate. This was a huge difference from NNPCR. We were also able to achieve higher CCR values as well, consistently ending anywhere between 85.0–92.0 %.

6.4.1 Effect of Hidden Nodes and Input Nodes

For all tests, we tested the effect of changing the number of hidden nodes from 3, to 5, and finally to 10 in each hidden layer. We received some surprising results, as it was dependent upon the training patterns used as opposed to finding a general pattern.

As shown in Fig. 6.1, increasing the number of hidden nodes for PA trace file generally had an increase in CCR. However, the increase was within hundredths of percents. The PA 3/10/10/1 case did gain quite a large increase in CCR, especially around the 700th epoch. All curves, however, seem to take a logarithmic curve to them.

Figure 6.2 demonstrates that unlike the other trace files, a low hidden node count for NY trace file was unable to stabilize. At this point, we generally say that the neural network was overgeneralizing and so the results may be able to stabilize if we turn down either momentum rate or learning rate. We can notice, however, that its counterparts, 3/5/5/1 and 3/10/10/1 had no trouble at all stabilizing around 90 %. Clearly, here, the conclusion would be to just increase the number of hidden nodes as opposed to tweaking the learning and momentum rates.

For the UC trace in Fig. 6.3, we noticed that around 250 epochs, there was a rather quick dip by about a tenth of a percent, similar to what occurred in the NY trace file in the 3/3/3/1 network around 100 epochs; however, in both of the UC cases (3/3/3/1 and 3/5/5/1), the neural network was able to stabilize again. Overall, altering the number of hidden nodes for the UC-test file had little to almost no effect on the CCR.

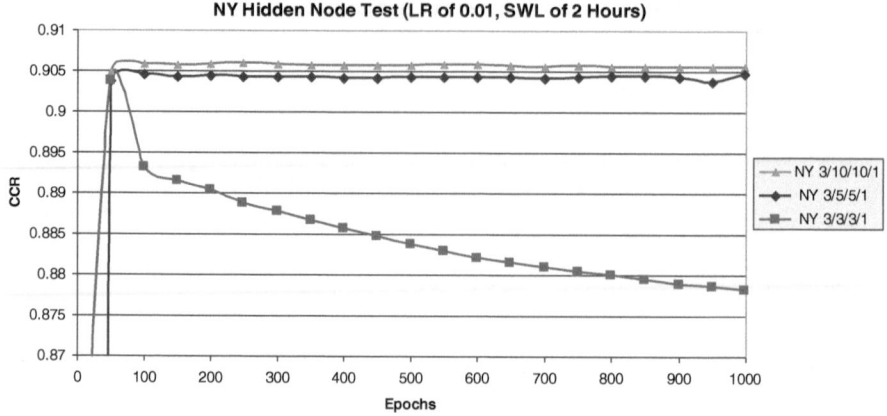

Fig. 6.2 Effect of hidden nodes for NY

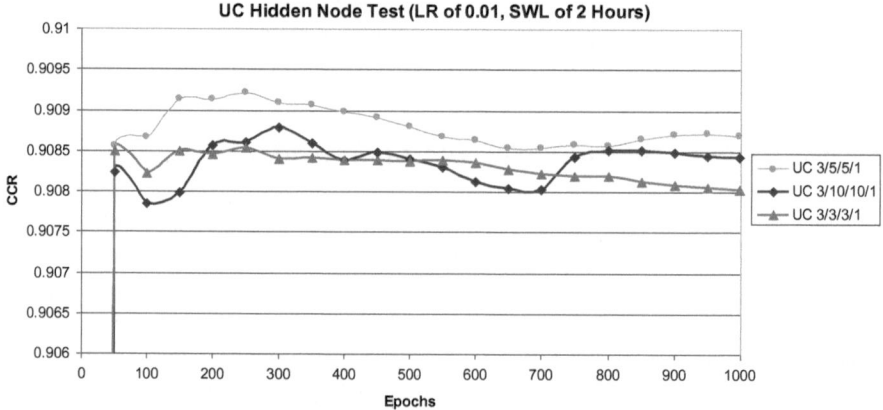

Fig. 6.3 Effect of hidden nodes for UC

By adding in the size input to the neural network structure, altering the hidden inputs had expected results for both UC and NY—that is, we can safely conclude generally increasing the number of hidden nodes increases the performance of NNPCR-2 during training. For the PA trace, it seems that the 4/5/5/1 network outperformed both the 4/3/3/1 and 4/10/10/1. In this case, by adding more hidden nodes, we have overgeneralized NNPCR-2. However, performance wise, it is off by a tenth of a percent, which in the long run is about ten or so patterns, a completely minuscule value.

Examining the differences in Figs. 6.4 and 6.7, there is actually an increase in CCR when we use *less* input nodes (ignoring the size input that is). This relationship is opposite when examining the increase in the number of inputs nodes for both the NY and UC trace file when we keep all other parameters constant.

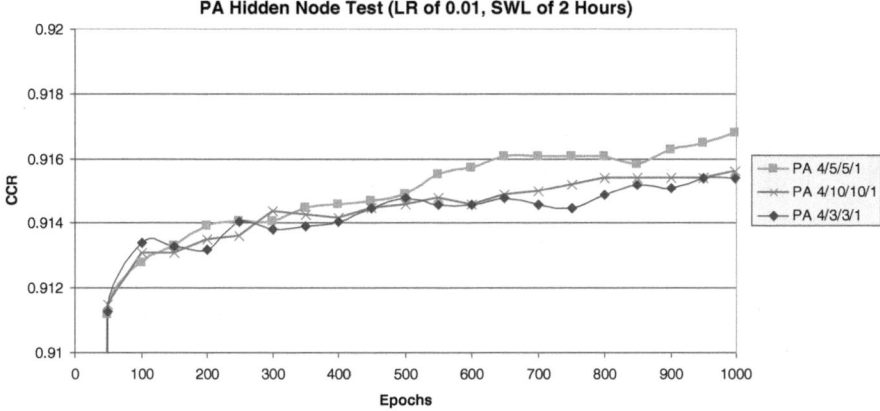

Fig. 6.4 Effect of hidden nodes for PA and four inputs

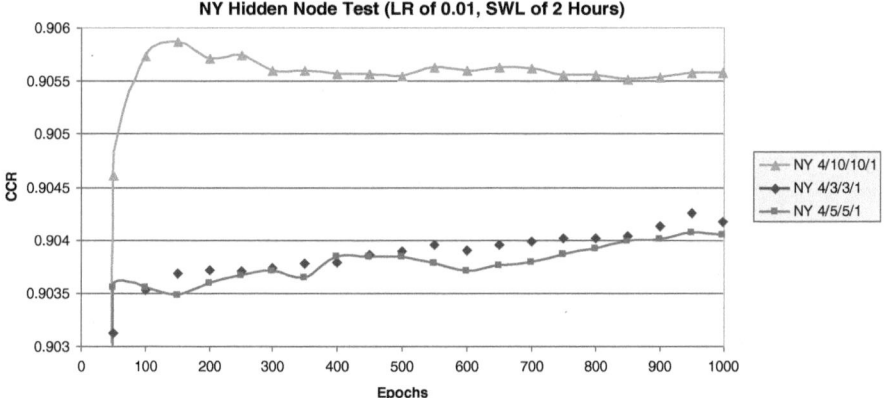

Fig. 6.5 Effect of hidden nodes for NY and four inputs

However, increasing the input nodes for a particular input only gains about a tenth of a percent for the UC and NY files, which is a couple hundred requests, respectively. As a rule of thumb using more inputs gains performance if there are a large quantity of patterns in the training set; more patterns allow the neural network to generalize on the third input—not enough patterns tends to lead the neural network in the wrong direction (Figs. 6.5 and 6.6).

6.4.2 Effect of the Sliding Window Length

The sliding window had some interesting results as well. While we performed 72 different instances of training the neural network with most of them testing the

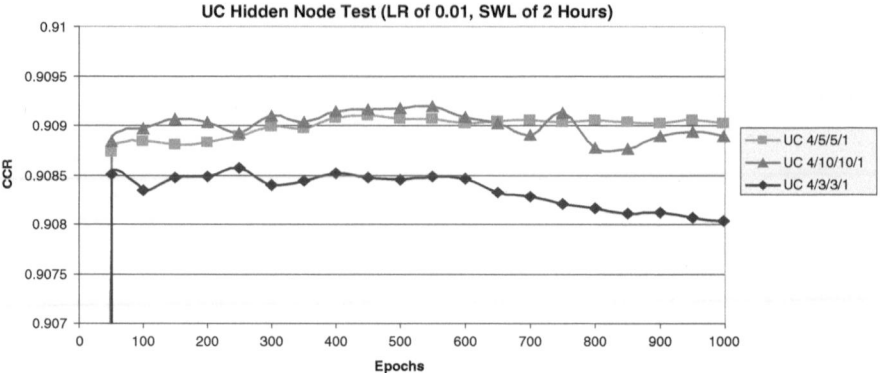

Fig. 6.6 Effect of hidden nodes for UC and four inputs

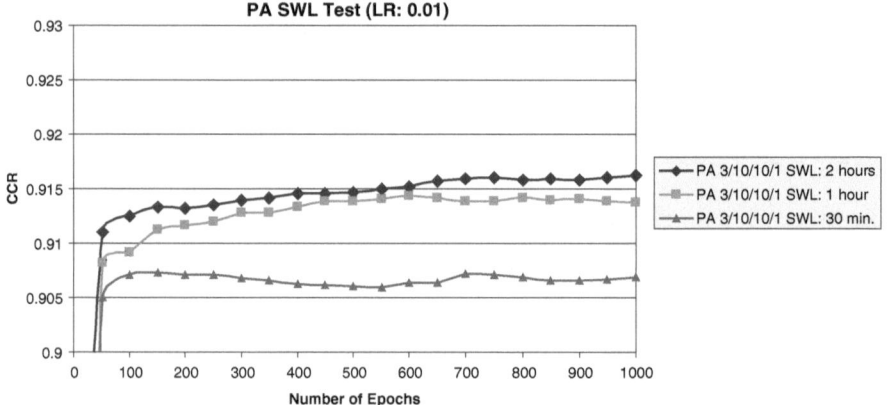

Fig. 6.7 Effect of SWL on PA 3/10/10/1

SWL, most of the results demonstrate the same relationship despite the parameters set. That is, as long as we keep the parameters constant, SWL has the same effect each time with those parameters. The following figures show only some of the tests we performed.

In Fig. 6.7, we see an interesting and rather large effect of the SWL on the 3/10/10/1 structure when trained on the PA trace. By decreasing the SWL, we actually lose performance by an entire percent (this correlates to a loss in classifying ∼90 patterns). It may have been an oddity, but we observed this exact same performance decrease when all other factors (LR, MR, and structure) stayed the same. Thus, for sparse request streams such as the PA, we observe the general relation that a smaller sliding window decreases training performance.

In terms of the UC and NY training files, however, we gained almost a 2 % performance increase in training when we dropped the SWL to a quarter of NNPCR trained with. Thus, on larger training sets, where the mean time between

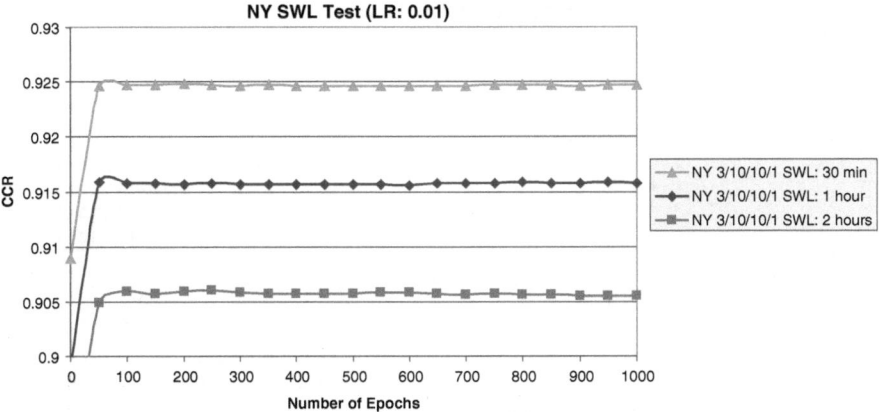

Fig. 6.8 Effect of SWL on NY 3/10/10/1

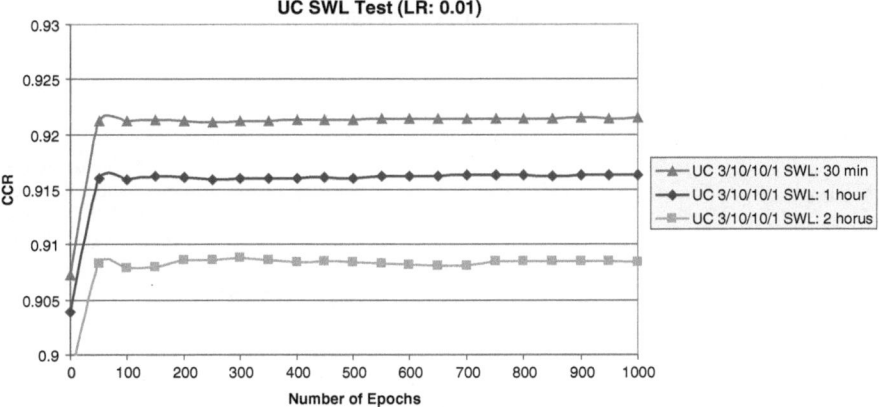

Fig. 6.9 Effect of SWL on UC 3/10/10/1

objects is much higher, decreasing sliding window length can actually increase performance. This may also allude to the fact that NNPCR-2 may be able to better handle denser request streams than sparse ones such as the PA-test case (Figs. 6.8 and 6.9).

6.4.3 Effect of the Learning Rate

To examine the effect of the learning rate on the neural network, we fixed all other parameters to what we found as their optimal value. This means for the PA NNPCR trainer, we used 3 input nodes (recency, frequency, and bias), three

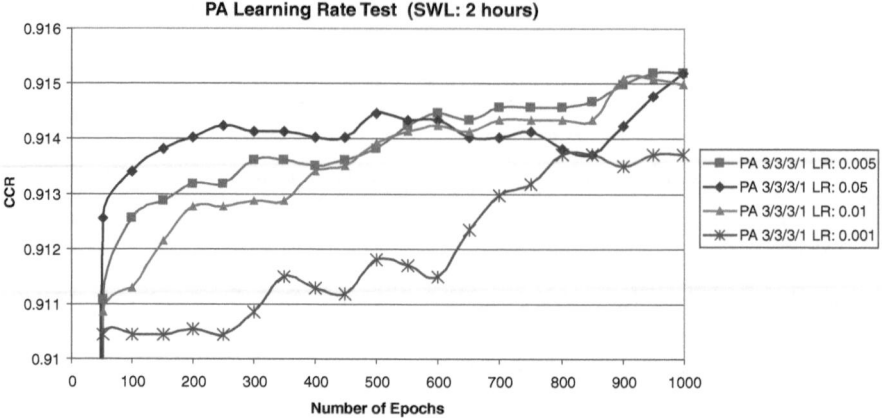

Fig. 6.10 Effect of learning rate on PA 3/3/3/1 structure

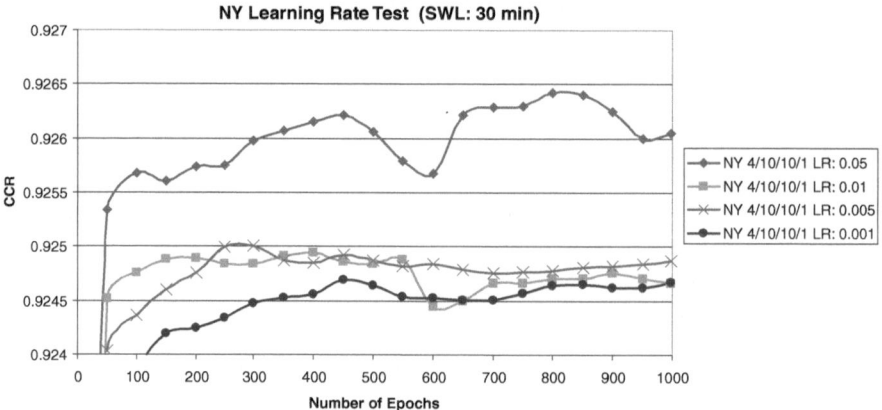

Fig. 6.11 Effect of learning rate on NY 4/10/10/1 structure

hidden nodes in each hidden layer, and SWL of two hours. For both UC and NY, we used the 4/10/10/1 structure with SWL of 30 min. Figures 6.13, 6.14, 6.15, 6.16 display the results of tweaking the learning rate at various levels (Figs. 6.10 and 6.11).

In large regards, the results were exactly as we expected with tweaking the learning rate. A higher learning rate would lead to a less stable or more random traversal of the error plane (seen clearest in Fig. 6.12 with the UC 4/10/10/1 LR: 0.05 case) yet would lead to achieving the performance metric faster. Decreasing the learning rate smoothed out this curve, yet, unexpectedly did not decrease the CCR for any of the cases by much. In fact, we did not see the changes in performance as we had witnessed previously with the SWL. Overall, then, it seems that while learning rate can affect how the neural net learns over time, it is generally better to go

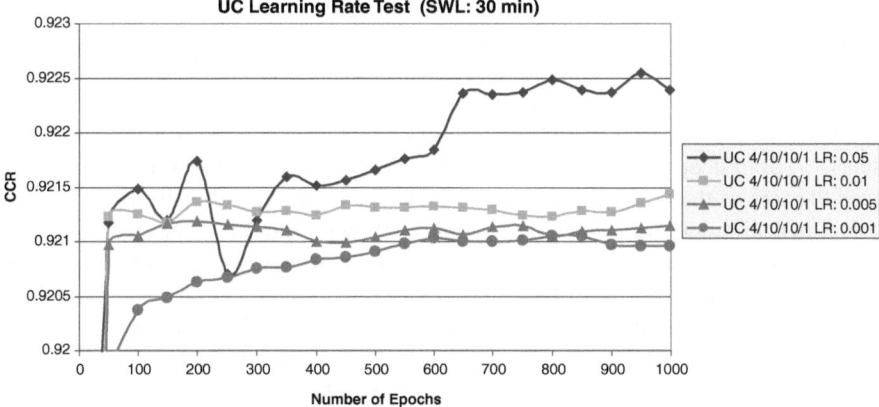

Fig. 6.12 Effect of learning rate on UC 4/10/10/1 structure

for a smoother traversal of the error plane. Thus, for our experiment/tests in the next section, we used the case where LR = 0.001.

6.5 Emulation Setup

Once our neural networks were trained and we verified our implementation in Squid, we ran several tests to measure the performance of how NNPCR-2 would fair against the other cache replacement strategies. We used two performance metrics, hit rate and byte-hit rate. To emulate the request streams recorded in the trace files, we used our own version of *wget* [8]. This version is similar to *wget* except it did *not* write the data it received from the network to a file. This was done mainly because we had very limited space restrictions and also to decrease the training time by the amount of disk latency.

Table 6.1 presents statistics about the three traces we used for this emulation. Non-cacheable requests were extracted from the files prior to our experiment as mentioned earlier. Each trace represented varying levels of temporal locality,

Table 6.1 Trace file statistics

Trace file location	Urbana-Champaign, Illinois (UC-test)	New York, New York (NY-test)	Palo Alto, California (PA-test)
Total requests	2,223,555	1,767,052	519,232
Cacheable requests	884,928 (39.79 %)	778,486 (44.06 %)	141,466 (27.24 %)
Total bytes	181.96 GB	21.65 GB	8.28 GB
Cacheable bytes	96.77 %	82.72 %	82.51 %
Unique objects	1,050,160 (47.23 %)	853,433 (48.29 %)	269,476 (51.90 %)
Cacheable objects	53.27 % of Above	54.02 % of Above	31.27 % of Above

spatial locality, total bandwidth, and number of requests testing the various limits of the replacement strategies. For both UC-test and NY-test, we used trace files spanning from April 3 to 9, 2008, and for the PA-test trace file, only an older set from July 19 to 25, 2007, was available at the time of this research.

Once our trace files were parsed, we first created all of necessary web objects that we would need for testing on a separate server from the web proxy server. We used the size of the request and the URI to designate unique objects. Then for each object in each trace file, we created a unique file with the same number of bytes as recorded in the trace. This process was done by essentially just filling up the file with as many newlines (\n) as there were bytes due to the fact that each character is a single byte. Once finished, we created a *wget* link file, which essentially is a flat file with a set of URIs that is requested in order one at a time.

There were two main issues with this approach, however. First, the files are requested one at a time, not asynchronously. Second, we could not control the timing of the requests so as to sync with the trace file durations, etc. This lead to our edited version of *wget* requesting the URIs as fast as it could on one thread, which leads to an entire week's worth of web requests to being finished in about 11 h of testing. Thus, certain characteristics of the request stream could not be replicated from the trace file into our emulation. Clearly, the recency values of requests/objects in our emulation did not sync up to what the recency values when the trace file was recorded. However, relative characteristics such as frequency and size would of course prevail in either testing environment.

In an attempt to correct the problem of correlating recency values as they would have been seen in the trace file (since the trace file is clearly an accurate model of the practical environment), we multiplied all durations, ΔT_i, by 25. This is equivalent to 1 week testing time/25 = 6.72 emulated testing hours; 6.72 h was close to the average total time that each link file completed within. In the implementation this means anytime that we needed to measure the amount of time that had passed since the last request occurred or the recency of an object, we would scale it by 25 times what was actually being reported.

Prior to running each test, we warmed up the cache with a smaller trace file from Boulder, Colorado. By using another trace file different from the others, we could guarantee that no files from that trace run would conflict with the other trace files. As a result, the cache would be filled by the time we started our simulation, putting our cache replacement strategies in effect immediately upon starting our tests. Therefore, all the results presented in Sect. 6.7 are the full results of the cache replacement strategy.

6.6 Emulation Results and Observations

We performed several different tests comparing different instances of NNPCR-2. We also compared NNPCR-2 with the other cache replacement strategies. Most results reported here have a standard deviation of error within 0.2 % for both

Table 6.2 Various instances of NNPCR-2 and their parameters

Test name	Structure	Training file	SWL
NNPCR4-UC	4/10/10/1	UC	30 min
NNPCR4-NY	4/10/10/1	NY	30 min
NNPCR3-UC	3/10/10/1	UC	30 min
NNPCR3-NY	3/10/10/1	NY	30 min
NNPCR3-PA	3/3/3/1	PA	2 h

metrics covered. Table 6.2 refers to the different parameters used for the various versions of NNPCR-2 tested. All NNPCR-2 tests used a max frequency of 128 and a size class of 22 (since we configured Squid to not cache objects larger than 8 MB as mentioned earlier). Overall, we found that the neural network trained with 4 inputs and UC testing file was the best instance of NNPCR-2 consistently on all trace files.

Since we used the implementation of the heap class in Squid, M-Metric was implemented in a non-optimal way. The Squid implementation of the heap only updates the key upon a cache hit or when the object is added into the heap. It does not update again otherwise. As a result, many keys become deprecated rather quickly in M-Metric, and objects which had high values keep those same values until an object is either requested again or finally removed from the cache. In this implementation, M-Metric thus suffers greatly from cache pollution and its performance is severely hindered. However, M-Metric for this research really served more as a lower bound to test NNPCR-2 against and as a way for us to validate our own implementation. Thus, we *expected* M-Metric to have the worst performance metrics in all testing simulations. If it did not, then we knew that somehow our implementation was invalidated.

In this chapter, we present the results of the Palo Alto tests. The New York and the Urbana-Champaign tests could be found in [9]. A summary of the results of PA-, NY-, and UC-tests are provided in Tables 6.3 and 6.4.

The following figures present the running analysis of the cache hit rate in relation to the number of requests fired at a certain point in the test. As we can see initially in Figs. 6.13 through 6.16, the graphs for different instances of NNPCR-2 and even other strategies have more or less the same shape for hit rate and byte-hit rate. We can see where at certain points in the emulation a large number of requests were made that statistically offered more to the cache hit rate. Large

Table 6.3 Summary of hit rate results

	LRU (%)	GDSF (%)	LFU-DA (%)	M-Metric (%)
PA	+2.57	−4.32	−0.46	+48.8
NY	+1.98	−8.67	+7.67	+40.0
UC	+5.1	−9.75	+0.817	+54.4
Average	+3.22	−7.58	+2.68	+47.6

Table 6.4 Summary of byte-hit rate results

	LRU (%)	GDSF (%)	LFU-DA (%)	M-Metric (%)
PA	+2.55	+16.25	−0.37	+45.0
NY	+5.03	+47.8	−1.98	+71.6
UC	+9.39	+54.7	−0.86	+72.4
Average	+5.66	+39.6	−1.07	+63.0

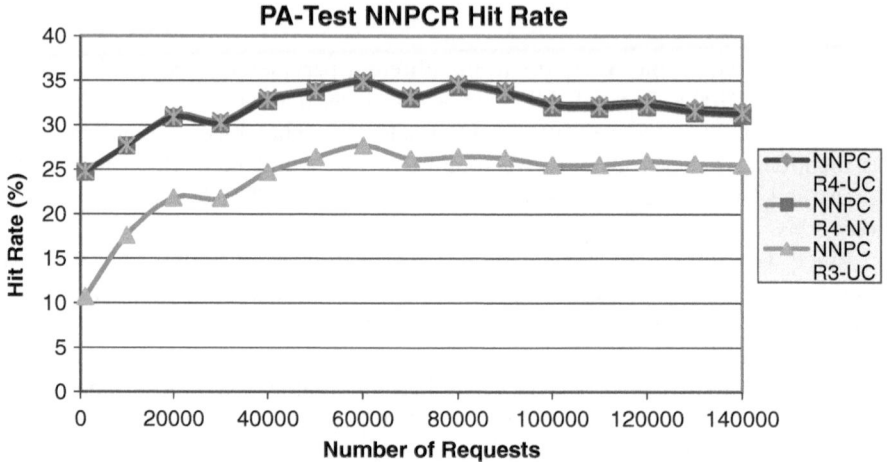

Fig. 6.13 PA-test hit rate results for different instances of NNPCR-2

jumps that occur in performance metrics at the same points are clearly demonstrating patterns in the request stream as opposed to the efficiency of the corresponding replacement strategy. However, despite the characteristics of the PA-test file, there is still a difference between strategies as shown in Figs. 6.15 and 6.16.

In terms of the comparison of the NNPCR-2 instances, as shown in Figs. 6.13 and 6.14, the performance metrics seem to always be relatively the same throughout—so close that due to their standard deviation of error, it is too close to call which instances are clearly doing better by examining these graphs alone. However, in the results we saw by doing multiple test runs, NNPCR4-UC always outperformed the others, even if it was not by much.

The worst performance of NNPCR-2 occurs with NNPCR3-UC. Clearly, the lack of input of the size of the object was a large drop in performance all around. This pattern occurred across all tests we ran. Despite the drop in performance, NNPCR3-UC has the same curvature as the other instances and is also a little more stable. Notice between 35,000 to about 50,000 requests that the other strategies are still rising in hit rate, while NNPCR3-UC flattens out.

When comparing NNPCR4-UC with the other strategies, we saw that LFU-DA had almost the same performance in hit rate and byte-hit rate (Figs. 6.15 and 6.16). LFU-DA outperforms NNPCR4-UC by approximately 0.2 % in both metrics. GDSF had the best hit rate, but as a result suffered in byte-hit rate. This is an

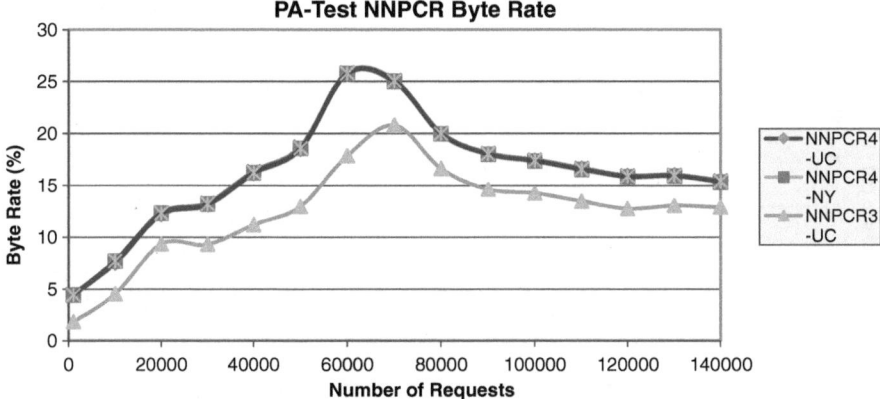

Fig. 6.14 PA-test byte-hit rate results for different instances of NNPCR-2

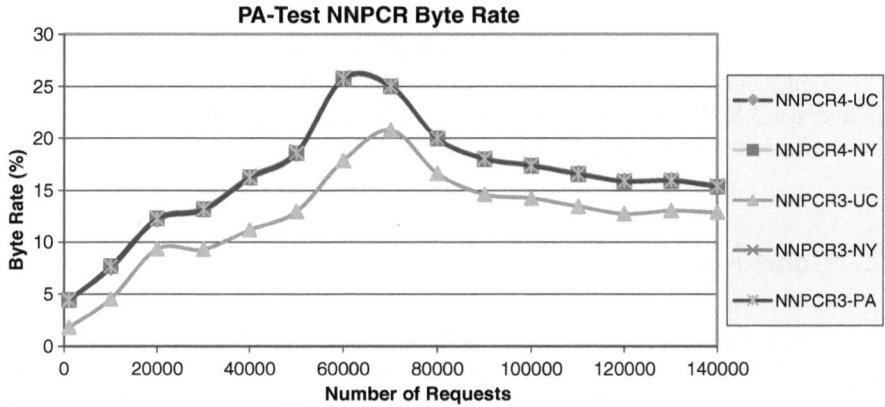

Fig. 6.15 PA-test hit rate results for different replacement strategies

expected effect due to GDSF's weighting toward smaller, frequently requested objects. Both LFU-DA and NNPCR4-UC had about a great balance between hit rate and byte-hit rate, where LRU followed incredibly close behind them in both metrics. As expected, M-Metric had the worst performance.

The most interesting observation is how the strategies except M-Metric had the same performance within the first 20,000 requests. This demonstrates all four of these strategies ability to pick up extreme changes after performing the Boulder-Colorado warm up phase. However, as the strategies deviate, we can see the differences in these strategies. Again, this pattern occurs not only in the Palo Alto test runs, but also New York and Urbana-Champaign.

We summarize the results of our tests in the following two tables. Table 6.3 shows the percentages of the average hit rate of NNPCR-2 as it compares to the four other strategies, LRU, GDSF, LFU-DA, and M-Metric for the three trace files

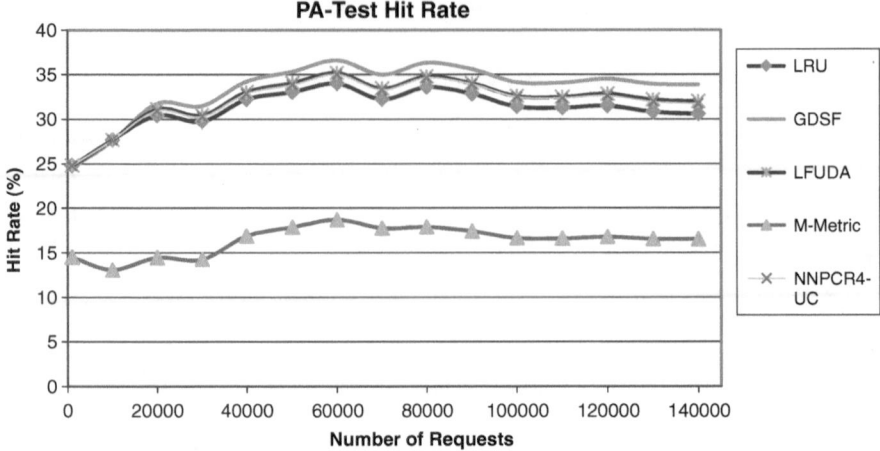

Fig. 6.16 PA-test byte-hit rate results for different replacement strategies

PA, NY, and UC. A "+" sign means that NNPCR-2 was on average better, and a "−" sign means that it was worse. For example, for PA trace file, NNPCR-2 was on average 2.57 % better than LRU and 4.32 % worse than GDSF. The last shows the averages over all traces. Table 6.4 shows similar results for byte-hit rate.

6.7 Conclusions

We implemented and tested NNPCR-2 in a real, practical web proxy cache framework. While NNPCR-2 may have not outperformed all the strategies, clearly NNPCR-2 was able to make better, balanced decisions than LRU and GDSF and had similar performance with LFU-DA. From our results, we see that NNPCR-2 is absolutely a plausible proxy cache replacement strategy. We have added an aging factor to NNPCR to deprecate objects from the cache in order to prevent cache pollution; this greatly improved NNPCR-2 and allowed it to run in an actual implementation for longer periods of time.

It was also shown that training NNPCR-2 is rather trivial, but multiple runs should always be done in order to find the correct sliding window length and other parameters to optimize NNPCR-2. We have also improved the training methods to gain an almost 5 % increase in CCR from NNPCR. Besides the odd case of NNPCR3-UC, the neural network can actually generalize from small training sets, such as Palo Alto, to larger ones such as New York and Urbana-Champaign.

Although we trained on a day's worth of patterns and emulated a week's worth of requests, NNPCR-2 may handle even larger training and testing sets. Training the neural network is trivial and once trained, NNPCR-2 requires no additional parameter tuning and handles changes in the request stream characteristics quite well. It is absolutely possible to provide default neural network structures and already trained configurations of NNPCR-2 to end users and system administrators in ready-to-use configurations.

References

1. M.F. Arlitt, L. Cherkasova, J. Dilley, R.J. Friedrich, T.Y. Jin Evaluating content management techniques for web proxy caches. ACM SIGMETRICS Perform. Eval. Rev. **27**, 3–11 (2000) (4 Mar)
2. J. Dilley, M. Arlitt, S. Perret, *Enhancement and Validation of Squid's Cache Replacement Policy, Internet Systems and Applications Laboratory, HP Laboratories*, Palo Alto, California, HPL-1999–69. May 1999
3. I. Tatarinov, *An Efficient LFU-like Policy for Web Caches*, Tech. Rep. NDSU-CSORTR-98-01, (Computer Science Department, North Dakota State University, Wahpeton, 1998)
4. C.C. Aggarwal, J.L. Wolf, P.S. Yu, Caching on the World Wide Web. IEEE Trans. Knowledge. Data Eng **11**, 94–107 (1999)
5. S. Romano, H. ElAarag, *A quantitative study of recency and frequency-based cache replacement strategies. Communication and Networking Simulation Symposium* (CNS2008), Spring Simulation Multiconference, Ottawa, pp 70–78 (2008)
6. IRCache Home, Available at http://www.ircache.net/
7. R.D. Reed, R.J. Marks, *Neural Smithing, Supervised Learning in Feedforward Artificial Neural Networks* (The MIT Press, Massachusetts, 1999), pp. 1–53
8. GNU Wget, Available at http://www.gnu.org/software/wget/
9. H. ElAarag, S. Romano, *Improvement of the Neural Network Proxy Cache Replacement Strategy, Communication and Networking Simulation Symposium* (CNS2009), Spring Simulation Multiconference, San Diego, CA, 22–27 Mar 2009